north carolina
state parks

A NICHE GUIDE

by Ida Phillips Lynch and Bill Pendergraft

*Although the authors and Niche Publishing LLC have tried to make this
information as accurate as possible, we accept no responsibility for any loss,
injury, or inconvenience sustained by anyone using this book.*

| N I C H E |

North Carolina State Parks: A Niche Guide

By Ida Phillips Lynch and Bill Pendergraft
Design by leesa brinkley graphic design, inc.

Published by Niche Publishing LLC
P.O. Box 9928
Chapel Hill, NC 27515-9928
www.nichepress.com

Library of Congress Control Number 2007938422

ISBN 0-9794591-0-9

ISBN 978-0-9794591-0-8

5 4 3 2 1

contents

acknowledgments

We would like to thank the staff of the North Carolina Division of Parks and Recreation for their cooperation and assistance in the development of our guide, especially Charlie Peek, public information officer for the division, who provided guidance and endured our incessant questions, and Lewis Ledford, division director, for his ongoing support of the project. Many superintendents, rangers, and others in the state parks system provided crucial information and encouragement, without which this guide would be much poorer.

We are grateful, too, to individuals from other organizations, both governmental and nonprofit, who contributed information: the North Carolina Natural Heritage Program, The Nature Conservancy, Friends of State Parks, and last but not least Carolyn Sakowski and Ed Southern at John F. Blair, Publisher, whose guidance during this project has been invaluable.

Many other people helped in the production of this book. Maura High, copy editor extraordinaire, turned our comma faults into compound and sometimes even complex sentences, and Leesa Brinkley converted a scramble of text and photographs into what we consider a thing of beauty. Ken Taylor took the cover photograph of Hammocks Beach State Park. The authors took most of the photos in the book except for those taken by N.C. State Parks staff and Jere Snyder and noted as such. We thank them for their lovely contributions. We would like to thank a variety of species for holding still.

Bill would like to thank his wife, Jeanne Phillips, for her tireless patience and support. Ida would like to thank her family and friends for their incredible support and good humor and for enduring her endless mantra: "I'm almost done with the book."

The many people who have helped us produce this guide are of course not responsible for any errors and omissions. That responsibility is fairly and squarely ours. We hope that the errors are few. But if you notice anything in the guide that could be corrected or improved – for that matter, if you found it interesting and helpful – we would love to hear from you. You can find our contact information on the Niche Publishing Web site, www.nichepress.com.

Ida Phillips Lynch and Bill Pendergraft

foreword

Since the state of North Carolina created its first state park on Mount Mitchell in 1916, the story of state parks has been about partnerships; partnerships to conserve the state's natural resources and to provide citizens with opportunities for education and recreation. Mount Mitchell, named after UNC professor Dr. Elisha Mitchell, was acquired with $20,000 appropriated by the state legislature. As one of the first state parks systems, North Carolina had an early start on protecting its treasured natural resources. In the decades following, generous landowners donated property that helped create additional parks. North Carolina made a major commitment to its state parks in 1993 with the passage of a $35 million bond referendum. Later, the creation of the Parks and Recreation and Clean Water Management Trust Funds and the growth of the Natural Heritage Trust Fund greatly enhanced the state parks' conservation and stewardship efforts. This funding has allowed the parks system to expand its partnerships with local governments, land trusts, businesses and the private sector.

As the state parks system has grown, the population of North Carolina has increased as well. And, so has the demand for more parks and more services in those parks. In 2002, more than 13 million people visited state parks, and the parks' popularity has not diminished. The system is in the midst of its strongest effort ever to expand existing parks and create new state parks through its *New Parks for a New Century* initiative. As of this date, four new parks and several state natural areas are being established. People are seeking more family-oriented activities and opportunities for environmental education and recreation. A growing number of organized groups are using state parks for newer types of recreation such as rock climbing, birding, mountain biking, kayaking and even marathons and triathlons. This timing for a new guide to state parks couldn't be better.

With the publication of *North Carolina State Parks: A Niche Guide,* North Carolinians and visitors alike have the first complete and portable guide to our parks that offers an overview of key features, spectacular photography and fascinating stories behind our state's natural wonders. We appreciate the continuing support of North Carolinians and guests in our state and we welcome the publication of this new guide.

Lewis Ledford, Director

NORTH CAROLINA DIVISION OF PARKS AND RECREATION

introduction

For a child hiking through deep forest or sitting by a campfire at night, the wild world may seem huge and limitless. But as people spend more time in wild places, their understanding deepens, and they begin to notice small things and the relations among them. The more one travels, the more one realizes that even in the most remote, wild areas of the world, there are limits to wilderness, and from that understanding comes a reverence for the symmetry of large, intact, wild places.

As North Carolina's population grows, its wild places are becoming increasingly important, not only as sanctuaries for wildlife, but as sanctuaries for ourselves. When we learn about the state's natural communities and experience them firsthand, we reconnect with the natural world and draw sustenance from it.

As of September 2007, North Carolina has more than 50 state parks, state natural areas, and state recreation areas, including several that are under development, all managed by the North Carolina Division of Parks and Recreation. The state park system continues to improve as new parks are added to the portfolio and existing parks are expanded. Since the mid-1990s, the park system has been developing modern visitor centers and exhibit halls in all the state parks with the support of the N.C. Parks and Recreation Trust Fund.

The division's mission is a complex one, but each part supports the others: to conserve and protect representative examples of the natural beauty, ecological features, and recreational resources of statewide significance; to provide outdoor recreational opportunities in a safe and healthy environment; and to provide environmental education opportunities that promote stewardship of the state's natural heritage.

This guidebook is the first in a series of *Niche Guides,* published by Niche Publishing LLC. It draws on the authors' rich personal experience with North Carolina's state parks and from their relationship and work with both the state parks system and the organization Friends of State Parks. The book updates the comprehensive 1989 guide *State Parks of North Carolina* by Walter C. Biggs Jr. and James F. Parnell, published by John F. Blair, Publisher. The authors have built on that pioneering work, providing basic information about North Carolina's state parks, recreation areas, natural areas, and new parks that are currently under development, which we call "Parks in Progress." The book does not include information about a few state natural areas that are managed as pure conservation lands because they are too fragile for intense visitation.

The three main sections of the guide provide contact information for each park, natural area, or recreation area; GPS coordinates for the latitude and longitude of the park office; the park's location with respect to nearby towns and highways (detailed directions are available on the Division of Parks and Recreation Web site at www.ncparks.gov); the park's size, as of January 1, 2007; the activities and amenities available; a general overview of special features of the park; a key safety tip or two; and a list of nearby natural areas to visit. Some state natural areas and parks in progress do not have contact information listed because they do not have facilities at this point in time and are not open to the public yet. Because a picture is worth a thousand words, each park description includes photographs chosen to capture a sense of the park's unique character and features. Some of the photographs are for sale at www.nichepress.com. The Web site also offers a video about North Carolina State Parks and information that we just could not squeeze into the book.

Many individuals and public and private conservation groups have played a critical role in protecting North Carolina's state parks. Space does not allow us to share all of these unique stories and recognize all of these dedicated people and organizations, so please refer to the information about Friends of State Parks and conservation organizations at the back of the book for general information about North Carolina's conservation community. You can get involved with state parks by joining Friends of State Parks and your local parks friends group and by supporting the work of the Division of Parks and Recreation and its partner organizations.

The guide does not include maps for the individual parks, as the most current maps of the parks, showing facilities and trails, are readily available on the Parks and Recreation Web site, www.ncparks.gov. This Web site contains links to other useful and continuously updated information, which will enrich your experience in the parks you visit, as well as your knowledge of the state's extraordinary biological diversity. For example, the site contains a comprehensive checklist of the plants and animals you might see at a particular park. Check the Web site before visiting a park to read about any closings due to inclement weather or construction. Mountain parks and roads are sometimes closed in the winter because of snow.

A printed guide to our parks is still needed in an age of Internet access: there is a place for a portable, advertising-free guide to parks for the glove compartment, backpack, or suitcase – a resource that doesn't require a plug or broadband access. We hope you will carry it on the trail and browse it on winter evenings. We are sensitive to the environmental impacts of printing, so we have printed this guide on recycled paper using vegetable-based inks.

If you have suggestions for revisions and additions to future editions of this guidebook, please e-mail us at the addresses on our Web site: www.nichepress.com.

We hope you enjoy your journey through North Carolina's state parks as much as we have.

help us keep this book up-to-date!

Outdoor enthusiasts will be glad to know that the North Carolina State Park system continues to improve as new parks are created, existing parks are expanded, and new visitor centers, trails, and other amenities are developed. These positive developments present a challenge for guidebook publishers. Our solution is to publish future editions of this book that reflect these ongoing developments. If you have any suggestions for changes and additions to future editions of this guidebook, please e-mail Bill Pendergraft and Ida Phillips Lynch at the e-mail addresses on our Web site: www.nichepress.com. If we use your suggestion in the next edition, you will receive full credit.

what's in the box?

Beneath the contact information for each state park, recreation area, and natural area in the book, you will see a box with other helpful information:

· **Location** – These general directions will guide you to the park from nearby towns and highways. You can find detailed directions and downloadable maps on the state parks Web site: www.ncparks.gov. Note that all state parks are featured on the official North Carolina highway map. When you are driving to a park, keep an eye out for brown state park signs that will direct you to the park.

· **Size** – The size refers to the property's acreage as of January 1, 2007.

· **GPS** – The GPS coordinates refer to the latitude and longitude of the park's office, or a central point of those natural areas without an office.

· **Activity icons** – The icons provide an overview of the amenities and activities available at the park and correspond to the legend below.

	Backpack camping		Marina access
	Bicycling		Nonmotorized boat access
	Canoe camping		Picnic shelter
	Dump station		Picnic tables
	Equestrian camping		Powerboat access
	Exhibit hall		Rental boats
	Fishing		Rock climbing
	Group cabins		Showers
	Group camping		Swimming
	Hang gliding		Tent camping
	Hiking		Tent, trailer, RV camping
	Historic site		Vacation cabins
	Horseback riding		Visitor center

mountains

Chimney Rock State Park

CHIMNEY ROCK STATE PARK
[PARK IN PROGRESS]

Hickorynut Gorge is one of those places in North Carolina that feels homey yet exotic at the same time. Here, granite domes loom over a narrow gorge that drops 1,800 feet in elevation. The Rocky Broad River runs through the gorge and empties into Lake Lure, a manmade reservoir ringed by vacation homes. This forested valley is home to spectacular rock formations, waterfalls, and rare animals like peregrine falcon. Tourists and celebrities have retreated here since the early 1900s and many movies, including *Dirty Dancing* and *Last of the Mohicans*, have been filmed in the area. When completed, the tentatively named Chimney Rock State Park will protect much of this singular landscape.

The latest development in the formation of Chimney Rock State Park came in 2007, when the State purchased 996-acre Chimney Rock Park for $24 million as an addition to the new state park. Chimney Rock had been a popular privately-owned attraction in the gorge since the early 1900s. The longtime owners of the park developed this mountaintop into a popular tourist attraction by making a rugged place accessible to people of all abilities. The

LOCATION	Rutherford County
SIZE	3,260 acres
GPS	35.4684, -82.2268

park's iconic 315-foot-tall rock spire offers a panoramic view of Hickorynut Gorge and Lake Lure. Visitors reach the spire by way of an elevator that climbs 26 stories through a rock face and deposits visitors in a nature center from where they can access a network of hiking trails.

Upon completion, the new state park will also feature 1,568-acre World's Edge, a natural area containing precipitous cliffs on the lip of the Blue Ridge Escarpment that was purchased by The Nature Conservancy and the Carolina Mountain Land Conservancy and transferred to the state. Other Nature Conservancy holdings, including an 850-acre tract on the north face of Rumbling Bald Mountain, a dramatic ridge overlooking a forested bowl, will also become part of the new state park.

Nearby
· South Mountains State Park: See page 62.
· DuPont State Forest: www.pisgahforest.com/public-lands/dupontstateforest/

ELK KNOB STATE PARK

The elk that inspired this peak's name has not been seen in the wild in North Carolina since the late 1700s, but hiking on Elk Knob still provides a sense of wandering into the past. The Nature Conservancy purchased 1,100 acres of the mountain in 2002 and later transferred the property to the Division of Parks and Recreation. It is one of the dozen mountains that ring the stunning Long Hope Valley – a high elevation valley that houses cranberry bogs, northern flying squirrels, and many rare plants. The amphibolite rock underpinning these peaks yields a nutrient-rich soil that feeds such rare plants as Gray's lily and large purple fringed orchid. Springs bubbling from the peak form the source waters of the North Fork of the New River.

At present, the only path to Elk Knob's 5,520-foot summit is a steep and rocky 1.25-mile former logging road. Hiking through the forests offers variety throughout the seasons: in wintertime you may find a rime-ice fairyland, and in summer grasses and trilliums carpet the understory. The trees become increasingly stunted the closer they are to the summit, until they end in a dwarf beech forest with 12-foot-tall trees carved by powerful ridgetop winds. A heath

CONTACT INFO

5564 Meat Camp Road
Todd, NC 28684
Phone: (828) 297-7261
Fax: (828) 297-7263
E-mail: elk.knob@ncmail.net

LOCATION   The park is about 9.5 miles north of Boone, off NC 194 in Watauga County.
SIZE   2,317 acres
GPS   36.3335, -81.6799

bald near the peak blazes with a variety of flowers in the summer, including brilliant flame azaleas.

You may observe the aerial antics of common ravens (which nest on the mountain) and soaring broad-winged hawks. During the breeding season a variety of neotropical migratory birds nest in the natural area, including chestnut-sided warbler, scarlet tanager, and black-throated blue and Canada warblers. The drumming of ruffed grouse often resonates in the woods in the nesting season, as does the rich, organ-like call of the veery.

You would be lucky to spot the elusive black bear, bobcat, and coyote that travel through this area, but keep an eye out for their scat and tracks. Several species of North Carolina's diverse salamanders inhabit the mountain's seeps, including slimy and pygmy salamanders.

On clear days, the perspective from the summit offers an unobstructed view of Long Hope Valley, and views of Bluff Mountain, The Peak, and Mount Jefferson, all in Ashe County, as well as Mount Rogers, Virginia's highest mountain. (The staff at Elk Knob also manages The Peak, the highest mountain in Ashe County.) Snake Mountain, another prominent Watauga County landmark, lies about one mile to the west of Elk Knob.

Staying Alive

Even on a balmy summer day, be prepared for any kind of weather, and make sure someone knows where you are hiking. Park staff recorded a wind-chill factor of minus 51°F in January 2007 at the bottom of the mountain.

Nearby

- Mount Jefferson State Natural Area: See page 20.
- New River State Park: See page 24.
- Three Top Mountain Game Land: www.ncwildlife.org

GORGES STATE PARK

Gorges State Park is located at the Blue Ridge Escarpment, a massive rocky spine that divides the mountainous Blue Ridge and low-lying Piedmont regions. This rock wall rises 2,000 feet in four miles and constitutes the divide between the Tennessee Valley and Atlantic drainages. Warm, moist air from the south flows over the escarpment and cools, dumping on average more than 80 inches of rain every year, making this one of the wettest places in eastern North America. Five whitewater rivers plunge over the escarpment, creating dramatic waterfalls.

CONTACT INFO

Highway 64
West Sapphire, Suite 3
Sapphire, NC 28774
Phone: (828) 966-9099
Fax: (828) 966-4526
E-mail: gorges@ncmail.net

The region is famous for its unusual plant life, as the greenhouse-like environment in the depths of the gorges harbors mosses, liverworts, and ferns that are found nowhere else, or are more typical of northern or even tropical climates. Up to 90 percent of the known populations of the rare Oconee bells, a close relative of galax, is found in the gorges. Bobcat and black bear range throughout this near-wilderness area, and many bird species, including at least 14 species of warblers, nest in the park. The state park is home to at least 11 salamander species, including the cryptically-colored green salamander.

LOCATION   Gorges State Park is 45 miles southwest of Asheville in Transylvania County and has two access areas: Grassy Ridge to the west and Frozen Creek to the east. Grassy Ridge, the main park entrance, is on NC 281 south of Sapphire. The Frozen Creek access is located on Frozen Creek Road, off US 64, eight miles east of Sapphire.

SIZE   7,443 acres

GPS   35.0888, -82.9198

In the 1990s Duke Energy sold more than 40,000 acres of land to conservation and natural resource agencies in the Carolinas, including the more than 7,000 acres comprising the state park. The park staff is working with the local community to develop a master plan that will provide a wilderness experience to a wide range of visitors while protecting ecologically sensitive areas.

Currently, hikers can choose from 24 miles of trails ranging from easy to strenuous. The 76-mile Foothills Trail runs from Table Rock State Park to Oconee State Park in South Carolina and passes across the North Carolina border into Gorges State Park; the trail is accessible from the Frozen Creek parking lot in Rosman. From the Grassy Ridge Access Area, you can backpack 2.7 miles to a primitive backcountry campsite, the Ray Fisher Place Campground, while RVers can drive along a 2.3-mile loop road from the visitor center to an RV campground with full amenities. Equestrians and mountain bikers can access the park from Frozen Creek and ride the 6-mile Auger Hole Trail. Anglers will want to wet a line in the park's rivers and streams, all of which are designated Wild Trout Waters.

Staying Alive
Hikers should stay on designated trails and be careful around steep waterfall areas.

Nearby
· Foothills Trail: www.foothillstrail.org
· Toxaway Game Land: www.ncwildlife.org
· Whitewater Falls: www.cs.unca.edu/nfsnc

LAKE JAMES STATE PARK

The 6,510-acre Lake James was created in the early 20th century by Duke Energy as part of a hydroelectric scheme along the Catawba River. The park was established in 1987, when the State of North Carolina purchased 564 acres of land from Crescent Resources, a subsidiary of Duke Energy. In 2005, the state purchased an additional 2,915 acres. With its expanses of clean water, views of the mountains in Pisgah National Forest, wildflowers, hiking trails, camp sites, and 150 miles of shoreline, the park is among the state's most visited.

Boating and fishing are a special focus at the lake, and boat ramps at Hidden Cove and Canal Bridge are open for powerboats, sailboats, canoes, and other craft. Fishing and waterskiing are popular pastimes at the park. Large and smallmouth bass are a prize here, along with bluegill, catfish, and muskellunge.

The 20 tent campsites are a short walk from the parking lot, and each site offers a fireplace with grill, picnic table, and camping area, and a nearby bathhouse is available to all campers. The camping areas connect to several miles of hiking trails that extend

CONTACT INFO
2785 Highway 126
Nebo, NC 28761
Phone: (828) 652-5047
Fax: (828) 659-8911
E-mail:
lake.james@ncmail.net

LOCATION   The park is located in Burke and McDowell Counties, five miles northeast of Marion on NC 126, just north of I-40 and Highway 70.

SIZE   3,514 acres

GPS   35.7292, -81.8882

along the isthmuses overlooking the lake. These short, easy one-way trails follow the lake shoreline to overlooks and offer fine views of the surrounding mountains and Linville Gorge. A sandy swimming beach is located near the park office.

The forests around the lake are home to typical Piedmont birdlife, such as eastern towhee and Carolina wren and some nice neotropical migrants in the spring and summer, including prothonotary warbler. Birders often check the lake from late fall to early spring for waterfowl such as ring-necked duck and bufflehead.

Staying Alive
Be sure never to swim alone, and swim only in designated areas.

Nearby
· Mount Mitchell State Park: See page 22.
· South Mountains State Park: See page 62.
· Blue Ridge Parkway: www.nps.gov/blri/
· Linville Falls Recreation Area:
  www.cs.unca.edu/nfsnc/recreation/wncwaterfalls/linvillefalls.htm
· Linville Gorge Wilderness Area: www.cs.unca.edu/nfsnc/recreation/linville.pdf
· Pisgah National Forest: www.cs.unca.edu/nfsnc/

MOUNT JEFFERSON STATE NATURAL AREA

hanks to a WPA-constructed two-mile paved road that climbs to just below the summit and features two overlooks, Mount Jefferson is a perfect destination for people of all ages and abilities. Rising 1,600 feet above the surrounding landscape, the peak towers over the towns of West Jefferson and Jefferson. The mountain offers a dramatic backdrop that changes with the seasons, from the pale to dark green succession of spring and summer to the frigid rime ice of winter. Mount Jefferson is part of the mountain chain that includes Elk Knob (see page 14) and The Nature Conservancy's Bluff Mountain; these mountains are underpinned with amphibolite rock, which produces soils that support diverse plant life.

Ambitious hikers and bikers can walk or bike to the summit, but most folks choose to drive. The forest on the summit's ridges and north-facing slopes has never been logged, and the relatively easy walk through these stunted gnarled oaks, shaped by strong northerly winds and winter ice storms, is a treat throughout the year. There are two trails: the 0.3-mile Summit Trail and the 1.1-mile roundtrip Rhododendron Trail, a self-guided

CONTACT INFO

1481 Mt. Jefferson
State Park Road
West Jefferson, NC 28694
Phone: (336) 246-9653
Fax: (336) 246-3386
E-mail:
mount.jefferson@ncmail.net

LOCATION   The natural area is on SR 1152, off US 221 Bypass between West Jefferson and Jefferson, in Ashe County.

SIZE   607 acres

GPS   36.4013, -81.4620

interpretive trail with markers and a trail guide. The Summit Trail leads to the mountain's highest point, at 4,683 feet, but you can get better views on nearby overlooks where you can see mountains in North Carolina, Tennessee, and Virginia on a clear day. A one-mile extension of the Rhododendron Trail should be open to the public by 2009.

The natural area is renowned for its plant life. Some of the spring bloomers include several species of trillium, pink lady's slipper, white bee-balm, jack-in-the-pulpit, and the common but lovely mayapple, with its umbrella-protected white flower. Migratory songbirds that nest here include Canada warbler, black-throated blue warbler, and chestnut-sided warbler. Listen for the memorable calls of the veery and wood thrush during spring and summer nesting season, and occasionally, the drumming of ruffed grouse. You may also see red-tailed hawks and ravens soaring over the mountaintop. If you hear chattering in the treetops, look for a red squirrel. The summit offers picnic tables and a rock picnic shelter with a fireplace.

Staying Alive
Hikers and picnickers on Mount Jefferson should be wary of uneven surfaces, slick rocks, unseen drop-offs, and changeable weather.

Nearby
- Elk Knob State Park: See page 14.
- New River State Park: See page 24.
- Stone Mountain State Park: See page 26.
- Blue Ridge Parkway: www.nps.gov/blri/

MOUNT MITCHELL STATE PARK

Established in 1916, Mount Mitchell State Park is North Carolina's first state park. Mount Mitchell is part of North Carolina's Black Mountains chain within the Appalachian Mountain range. These mountains are much older than the Rockies to the west; 250 million years ago the ancient rocks were thrust upward, and over the millennia since then have slowly eroded to form the gentle profiles we see today. At 6,684 feet above sea level, Mount Mitchell is the highest point east of the Mississippi.

CONTACT INFO

2388 State Highway 128
Burnsville, NC 28714
Phone: (828) 675-4611
Fax: (828) 675-9655
E-mail:
mount.mitchell@ncmail.net

Natural communities established during the frigid Pleistocene era survived on the area's highest peaks as the climate began to warm almost 12,000 years ago, so many of the plants and animals found in the park are more characteristic of alpine areas farther north. Look for rhododendron, yellow birch, mountain ash, and beech. June through September is the time to see wildflowers in bloom, including St. John's wort, mountain aster, purple turtlehead, and common yarrow. The park's high-elevation spruce-fir forest is under siege: research suggests that acid precipitation is weakening the trees and making them increasingly susceptible to severe

LOCATION   The park is off NC 128 and the Blue Ridge Parkway, 33 miles northeast of Asheville, in Yancey County.

SIZE   1,946 acres

GPS   35.7624, -82.2678

weather and insect damage, particularly the balsam woolly adelgid. Native to Central Europe, this exotic pest injects a toxin into the firs, blocking the path of nutrients through the tree.

Red squirrel, woodchuck, black bear, and gray fox may be spotted at Mount Mitchell. More than 90 bird species have been observed here, including northern saw-whet owl and red crossbill. A good way to hear owls calling is to camp at the park in May and June.

The park offers more than 43 miles of hiking trails, many strenuous. Hikers who want to scale Mount Mitchell take the challenging 6-mile Mt. Mitchell Trail, which requires an all-day commitment (about eight hours for fit hikers). The Balsam Trail is open for horseback riding. Primitive and family tent camping is available in the park. A new observation tower on the summit was under construction as this book went to press.

Staying Alive

The winter on Mount Mitchell can be brutal, with below-freezing temperatures and blowing snow, and while the park is open all year, May 1 to October 31 is considered "the season" by park staff. The Blue Ridge Parkway, too, is sometimes closed in winter due to ice and snow. To find out about road closures and weather conditions on the Blue Ridge Parkway, call (828) 298-0398 or visit www.nps.gov/blri/. For trail closures and information, contact the Appalachian Ranger District at (828) 682-6146 or visit www.cs.unca.edu/nfsnc/.

Nearby

- Pisgah National Forest: www.cs.unca.edu/nfsnc/
- Mountains to Sea Trail: www.ncmst.org
- Blue Ridge Parkway: www.nps.gov/blri/

NEW RIVER STATE PARK

Older than the surrounding Appalachian mountains, and unusual in that it flows north, the New River winds from North Carolina through southwestern Virginia and West Virginia and a series of dams into the Kanawha and Ohio Rivers and ultimately into the Mississippi. The river is believed by some to be the oldest in North America, and second in age only to the Nile.

In 1965 the Appalachian Power Company wanted to dam the river for water storage. Citizens and government agencies opposed the project, and after 10 years of legal battles, the North Carolina General Assembly declared 26.5 miles of the river extending to the Virginia state line a State Scenic River. Administrative responsibility for this section of river was given to the N.C. Division of Parks and Recreation. A year later the Department of the Interior named the New a National Wild and Scenic River, and the state park was established in 1977.

The New is known around the world for its paddling, and its small rapids and beautiful scenery of farms, meadows, and forests make it a perfect destination for paddlers of all ages and abilities.

CONTACT INFO

US 221 Access
Jefferson, NC 28640
Phone: (336) 982-2587
Fax: (336) 982-3943
E-mail: new.river@ncmail.net

LOCATION New River State Park is made up of several parcels of land along the New River in Ashe and Alleghany Counties, east of the town of Jefferson, and north of US 221 and NC 88. There are multiple points of access to the park, some of which can be accessed only by canoe or kayak. Those accessible by vehicle are the Wagoner Road Access Area off SR 1590, where the park office is located, the US 221 Access Area, and the Kings Creek Access Area off US 16. Park signs are at all major turns. For detailed directions and a map, visit the state parks Web site, www.ncparks.gov.

SIZE 2,339 acres

GPS 36.4638, -81.3425

Oak-hickory forests rise above an understory of sourwoods and sassafras, and you are likely to see mink and river otter along the way, with an occasional osprey circling above. Springtime brings a profusion of wildflowers such as trillium and Dutchman's breeches. During spring and summer you can see an abundance of nesting birds, including rough-winged swallow, ovenbird, and hooded warbler. The river is full of water and wading birds, including wood duck and hooded merganser. The fishing is also excellent: the river provides some of the best smallmouth and redeye bass fishing in the region, and sections of the river and tributary streams are stocked with muskellunge and rainbow and brown trout.

In May 2007, the park opened a new 14,000-square-foot visitor center with an exhibit hall, as well as an improved campground at the US 221 Access. Several local outfitters rent canoes and tubes and often provide transportation. For more information, contact the park office, or the Ashe County Chamber of Commerce at www.ashechamber.com or (888) 343-2743, or the Alleghany County Chamber of Commerce at www.sparta-nc.com/ or (800) 372-5473.

Staying Alive
Paddlers should always wear a personal flotation device on the water and portage around low bridges. Make sure you know the current river conditions before you head out.

Nearby
· Mount Jefferson State Natural Area: See page 20.
· Stone Mountain State Park: See page 26.
· Bluff Mountain Nature Preserve: nature.org/northcarolina
· Doughton Park along the Blue Ridge Parkway: www.nps.gov/blri/

STONE MOUNTAIN STATE PARK

"**M**onadnock" is a winning word for your next Scrabble game, scoring 18 points by itself, plus any accruing extra points you can finagle, and Stone Mountain is the largest plutonic igneous monadnock (39 points) in the state and perhaps in the eastern United States. Located just south of the Blue Ridge Parkway, this granite dome is 2,305 feet above sea level and juts 600 feet above its base. The rock was formed from magma and became exposed and isolated as the surrounding less resistant rock eroded over time. The best views of Stone Mountain are from Stone Mountain Overlook and at Devil's Garden Overlook, outside the park along the Blue Ridge Parkway.

CONTACT INFO

3042 Frank Parkway
Roaring Gap, NC 28668
Phone: (336) 957-8185
Fax: (336) 957-3985
E-mail:
stone.mountain@ncmail.net

In addition to the massive stone dome, this beautiful park boasts waterfalls; native brook trout streams; cove forest with red maples, oaks, sweet birch, and Canada hemlock; and chestnut oak forest on open slopes and ridgetops. In the chestnut oak forest, look for little sprouts of what's left of the blighted American chestnut. Wildlife that you would expect in the Piedmont, including wild turkey and migratory songbirds, inhabit the area. Keep an eye peeled for ravens that often soar overhead.

LOCATION Stone Mountain State Park is located seven miles southwest of Roaring Gap, in Wilkes and Alleghany Counties. It can be reached from I-77 and US 21, or from NC 18.

SIZE 14,119 acres

GPS 36.3873, -81.0273

The park offers excellent trails for hiking, backcountry camping, and horseback riding, along with historic structures. Hutchinson Homestead offers a lesson on mid-19th-century farming life, and Garden Creek Baptist Church, built about 1897, still holds services from May through October.

A sampling of the park's 16 miles of trails includes the strenuous 4.5-mile Stone Mountain Loop Trail that leads hikers to the summit of the mountain and to the top of Stone Mountain Falls. The Middle and Lower Falls Trails take hikers to other scenic falls, and the Widows Creek Trail follows a waterway to the backcountry camping sites. The Mountains to the Sea Trail also runs through the park. Most of the park's trailheads are on the southern side of Stone Mountain. Experienced rock climbers can climb in designated areas if they get a permit from the park office.

Staying Alive
Stay on the trails; going off the trail on top of Stone Mountain itself can be very dangerous because there are slippery spots on the rock. Any rocks that are dislodged on the mountain can harm people below.

Nearby
- Mount Jefferson State Natural Area: See page 20.
- Blue Ridge Parkway: www.nps.gov/blri/

piedmont

Medoc Mountain State Park

CROWDERS MOUNTAIN STATE PARK

Two peaks – Kings Pinnacle and Crowders Mountain – are the focal points of this state park and are all that remains of a mountain range over 450 million years old. Kings Pinnacle rises 1,705 feet above sea level, and has a rounded profile, while Crowders Mountain, which rises to 1,625 feet, is distinguished by its 100- to 150-foot-high vertical cliffs. The park exists today because the kyanite-quartzite rock from which these mountains are made is resistant to erosion, and because local citizens fought to preserve them against the threat of commercial exploitation.

CONTACT INFO

522 Park Office Lane
Kings Mountain, NC 28086
Phone: (704) 853-5375
Fax: (704) 853-5391
E-mail: crowders.mountain@
ncmail.net

The gold rush came to this area in the early 1800s, when huge nuggets of gold were found in the area. Kyanite, a mineral used to make spark plugs, was also mined nearby. In the 1970s, when Crowders Mountain was threatened, the Gaston County Conservation Society and others spearheaded an effort to save the land from strip-mining, and the park opened in 1974, and continued to expand in the years that followed. In 2000, an additional 2,000-acre segment of land was added to the park, which connects to Kings Mountain National Military Park and Kings Mountain State Park in South Carolina.

LOCATION	Crowders Mountain State Park is a short distance from I-85, in Gaston County, 25 miles west of Charlotte, and close to the state line.
SIZE	5,126 acres
GPS	35.2127, -81.3006

The park offers 12 miles of trails through varied habitats, including some easy walks around the lake, and others that climb to the summits of Crowders Mountain and Kings Pinnacle and offer vantage points to view the surrounding landscape. Look in the park's streams for water-loving creatures like pickerel frog and northern cricket frog. Boggy places are home to dusky and two-lined salamanders. More than 160 bird species have been recorded in the park, including waterfowl, wading birds, hawks, and songbirds.

Backcountry and group camping is available, and experienced climbers may climb in designated areas. Climbers must register with the park office. A nine-acre manmade lake offers canoe rentals and fishing, but no swimming or private boats are permitted.

Staying Alive
The greatest natural hazards here are the steep cliff faces. Stay on the designated trails, at a safe distance from the cliff edge. Climbers must follow the park's regulations concerning climbing technique and safety; you can check these on the park's Web site.

Nearby
· Kings Mountain State Park, Blacksburg, South Carolina: www.southcarolinaparks.com

DEEP RIVER STATE TRAIL
[PARK IN PROGRESS]

The Deep River flows steadily through the Piedmont mosaic of agricultural lands, small towns, and forest. The river rises near High Point and flows eastward through several counties until it merges with the Haw River near Moncure in Lee County and forms the Cape Fear, one of the state's most important rivers. The Deep has long been a popular waterway among paddlers and anglers and now a conservation partnership is creating more ways for people to enjoy the river. In August 2007, the North Carolina General Assembly authorized adding the Deep River State Trail to the State Parks System. According to the N.C. Division of Parks and Recreation (NCDPR), the trail will probably begin as a canoe/paddle trail with a series of public access sites and could eventually grow into a regional land and water trail that connects to Greensboro, the N.C. Zoological Park, and Jordan Lake.

Biologists and conservation groups consider the Deep to be nationally significant because it is home to rare aquatic species such as the Cape Fear shiner, a minnow; the Carolina redhorse, a variety of "quillback" fish; and several species of rare mussels. As well, the river provides drinking water for Chatham and Lee

LOCATION   Chatham, Guilford, Lee, Moore, and Randolph Counties

Counties. Paddling on the river is a delight, as much of it is wide and slow-moving, offering a relaxing way to watch raptors soaring overhead, fish breaking on the surface, and turtles basking on snags.

The Deep River region is rich in human history, featuring historic sites like House in the Horseshoe, an 18th-century plantation; remains of a failed canal and lock system; and Endor Iron Furnace, a 35-foot-high Civil War-era brownstone structure that looms over the river floodplain. Triangle Land Conservancy (TLC), a nonprofit regional land trust, has worked closely with NCDPR to develop the Deep River State Trail and has protected several key natural areas along the river, including 426 acres surrounding Endor Iron Furnace, and White Pines Nature Preserve, a natural area with an unusual grove of white pines and other mountainous species. TLC and state-owned properties could eventually be utilized as the first public access areas on the state trail.

ENO RIVER STATE PARK

W hether you are paddling the Eno's rapids or hiking its trails, Eno River State Park takes you on a journey through the natural and cultural history of piedmont North Carolina. The park is a corridor for both people and wildlife through a built-up and congested section of the central piedmont. In spite of intense development surrounding the park, one can find peaceful sanctuary along this river.

The Eno originates in northwest Orange County and flows eastward for approximately 33 miles before merging with the Little and Flat Rivers to form the Neuse, which ultimately flows into Falls Lake. Although repeatedly logged, beautiful old bottomland hardwood forests still border the river; you will find tulip poplar, sweet gum, and river birch among the trees there. Wildlife typical of urban areas (such as white-tailed deer and raccoons) can be found here, along with barred owls, great blue herons, wild turkeys, and wood ducks.

Approximately 21 miles of generally moderate hiking trails traverse the park and its diverse habitats, and take hikers past mountain

CONTACT INFO

6101 Cole Mill Road
Durham, NC 27705
Phone: (919) 383-1686
Fax: (919) 382-7378
E-mail: eno.river@ncmail.net

LOCATION Eno is a linear park that follows the river from Hillsborough in Orange County toward Falls Lake in Durham County. The park has five access areas: Few's Ford, Pleasant Green, Cabe Lands, Cole Mill, and Pump Station. The park office is located in the Few's Ford area off Cole Mill Road (SR 1569), which can be reached from I-85.

SIZE 3,917 acres

GPS 36.0540, -78.9848

laurel-covered bluffs and the historic sites of mills, wagon fords, and swimming holes. Some of the park's most beloved hikes include the Cox Mountain Trail, which offers a fairly steep climb to a scenic hardwood forest and back into the river floodplain, and the Bobbitt's Hole Trail, which passes by one of the prettiest bends in the river. More than 30 mills, primarily saw and grist mills, were once located along the river and helped sustain lively communities in this area prior to the demise of the mill era in the mid-1800s.

Paddling is popular along the Eno, and the river offers Class I, II, and III rapids. Launch at Few's Ford, Pleasant Green, and Cole Mill. The best rapids are between Hillsborough and Roxboro Roads in Durham. River travel is easiest when the water level is high, so check conditions at the park office to avoid portaging. Check the Eno River Association Web site for river levels (www.enoriver.org). You can fish here for largemouth bass and crappie.

Group and primitive camping can be arranged through the park office.

continued next page

Occoneechee Mountain State Natural Area

A satellite of Eno River State Park, Occoneechee Mountain State Natural Area is one of the Triangle's most important natural areas and is a prominent landmark along I-85 as it rises to 867 feet above sea level. This isolated monadnock is the highest point between Hillsborough and the coast. Hike the trail to the summit to see an unparalleled view of the Eno River Valley and historic Hillsborough.

One of the most undisturbed chestnut oak forests remaining in the Triangle cloaks the summit. Researchers believe that plant and animal life on the mountain's north-facing slopes has remained unchanged since the last ice age, as the brown elfin butterfly, typically found 100 miles to the west, still resides in this elevated area, as well as Catawba rhododendron, which grows on rocky outcrops.

This area was home to the Occaneechi band of the Saponi Nation. Learn more at www.occaneechi-saponi.org.

Staying Alive

If you are boating on the river, wear a life jacket and check with the park office about water conditions. No swimming is allowed in Eno River State Park.

Nearby

- Falls Lake State Recreation Area: See page 38.
- Jordan Lake State Recreation Area: See page 44.
- William B. Umstead State Park: See page 64.
- Duke University's 7,000-acre research and teaching forest, Duke Forest, offers great hiking and nature study throughout the year. Visit www.dukeforest.duke.edu, where you can also purchase a copy of *The Duke Forest at 75: A Resource for All Seasons*, by Niche Publishing's Ida Phillips Lynch.

Eno River Association

Without the tireless work of the Eno River Association and the efforts of its founders, Margaret and Holger Nygard, the Eno would now be a Durham County reservoir. In 1966, the Durham Department of Water Resources proposed a reservoir for the Eno River Valley, but the plans were scuttled in 1973 after great pressure from the association and others. The association and The Nature Conservancy, North Carolina Chapter, worked to conserve more than 1,000 acres that would become the park.

The Eno River Association is dedicated to conserving and protecting the nature, culture, and history of the Eno River basin. Each July the association hosts Festival for the Eno, a fundraiser at West Point on the Eno featuring food, performing and visual arts, and more. Visit www.enoriver.org for more information.

FALLS LAKE STATE RECREATION AREA

F alls Lake was created in 1981 when the U.S. Army Corps of Engineers dammed the Neuse River. The lake now covers the falls that once tumbled from the piedmont into the coastal plain and offers handy retreat for people in the Triangle region. The recreation area consists of seven separate parks (Beaverdam, B. W. Wells, Highway 50, Holly Point, Rolling View, Sandling Beach, and Shinleaf), primarily located on the eastern shore of the lake. Visit the park office or state park Web site for directions and maps of each site. The recreation areas offer a range of facilities: some have camping areas (with hot showers), and others have boat ramps, fishing piers, and picnic areas and shelters.

Falls Lake offers many activities for both aquatic and terrestrial types. Water-lovers can swim at sandy beaches, paddle in canoes or kayaks, sail, or speed around in motorized boats. The Division of Parks and Recreation has teamed up with Triangle-area fat-tire bike enthusiasts to develop approximately 14 miles of single-track mountain-biking trails (ranging from beginner to advanced) in the Beaverdam area. Call the park office for current conditions, and/or visit www.trianglemtb.com to see trail conditions and download maps.

CONTACT INFO

13304 Creedmoor Road
Wake Forest, NC 27587
Phone: (919) 676-1027
Fax: (919) 676-2954
E-mail: falls.lake@ncmail.net

LOCATION   The recreation area falls in three counties: Durham, Wake, and Granville. The office is on NC 50, one mile north of the intersection of NC 98, just before the bridge over the lake.

SIZE   5,035-acre recreation area (Falls Lake overall comprises a 12,000-acre lake and 26,000 acres of woodlands).

GPS   36.0072, -78.6806

Volunteers are helping construct the North Carolina Mountains to Sea Trail, which will ultimately extend more than 900 miles from the Great Smoky Mountains to Jockey's Ridge State Park on the Outer Banks. A 34-mile section of the trail, the Falls Lake Trail, runs through the recreation area and will eventually cover about 50 miles along the lake's southern shoreline. For more information visit www.ncmst.org.

The recreation area's open lake waters, flats, and hardwood forest offer a wealth of opportunities for birders and naturalists. The upper end of the lake, which is wider and shallower than the lower end, offers good birding for shorebirds and wading birds. The lake is a good spot to look for bald eagles throughout the year and huge flocks of gulls in the winter. While birding or paddling along the edges of the lake, keep an eye out for river otter and muskrat.

Staying Alive
Swimming is allowed only in designated areas and no lifeguards are on duty in these areas. Falls Lake is big water, and large waves can develop during high wind. If you are boating on the lake, wear an approved flotation device.

Nearby
· Eno River State Park: See page 34.
· Jordan Lake Recreation Area: See page 44.
· William B. Umstead State Park: See page 64.

Close to the Triad area of the state, and north of Winston-Salem, Hanging Rock State Park is located at the eastern end of the isolated Sauratown Mountain range. The park boasts a great diversity of landscapes, from rock escarpments and outcrops to cascading waterfalls and quiet streams, and offers a host of recreational activities from rock climbing to swimming.

The visitor center provides an overview of the park's natural and cultural history, which includes the construction of the stone buildings in the park by the Civilian Conservation Corps (CCC), from 1935 to 1942. The Corps also built a dam on Cascade Creek in 1938, creating a lovely 12-acre lake, with a bathhouse that is listed on the National Register of Historic Places.

CONTACT INFO

2015 Hanging Rock Park
Road North
Danbury, NC 27016
Phone: (336) 593-8480
Fax: (336) 593-9166
E-mail:
hanging.rock@ncmail.net

Twelve trails covering 18 miles give hikers a wealth of choices. Most visitors take short trails to see the waterfalls, and many hike the 1.2-mile trail to the top of Hanging Rock. The trails range from easy to strenuous and lead hikers to expansive views and rock-climbing walls. The Hanging Rock Trail and Moore's Wall Loop Trail offer panoramic views of the surrounding landscape at their summit

LOCATION   The park lies off NC 8, four miles northwest of Danbury, in Stokes County.
SIZE   7,043 acres
GPS   36.3979, -80.2574

points. Moore's Knob is the highest point in the park, at 2,579 feet. Rock climbing is available at Cook's and Moore's Walls, with cliffs up to 400 feet high. Climbing is free, but climbers must stay in designated areas and register with the park staff.

Seventy-three camping sites are available for tents and trailers in addition to eight group camping sites. The park is unique in offering cabin rentals for people who make reservations through the park office. Before visiting the park, call the office to check on cabin availability. Each of the 10 cabins houses up to six people and includes two bedrooms, a kitchen, and living room. One cabin is handicapped accessible.

Staying Alive
Hikers are warned to stay away from cliff faces and waterfalls. Rock climbers must register at the park office and use appropriate climbing equipment and protocols. One should never climb alone.

Nearby
- Pilot Mountain State Park: See page 58.
- Sauratown Trail: The Sauratown Trail is a 35-mile section of the North Carolina Mountains to Sea Trail, which links Hanging Rock to Pilot Mountain State Park. The trail is open to hikers and horse riders. Visit www.sauratowntrails.org.

HAW RIVER STATE PARK

[PARK IN PROGRESS]

The N.C. Division of Parks and Recreation continues to refine its plans for this water and land-based park that was authorized in 2003 and will consist of land along the Haw River on the Guilford-Rockingham County line. The Summit Conference Center, located within the state park, is already open to the public. The State purchased this property from the Episcopal Diocese of North Carolina in 2005 and the conference center is available for rent by public and private group activities such as conferences, training events, and youth retreats. The center can accommodate 180 overnight guests and 300 day-use visitors and provides meeting spaces, motel and dormitory sleeping facilities, recreation facilities, and a dining room.

In other conservation work along the Haw River, the State is developing the Haw River Trail, a multi-use trail that will link Haw River State Park to Jordan Lake State Recreation Area about 70 miles to the south. The trail will also tie into the Lower Haw River State Natural Area (see page 50).

Nearby
· Hanging Rock State Park: See page 40.

CONTACT INFO

The Summit at Haw River
State Park
339 Conference Center Drive
Browns Summit, NC 27214
Phone: (336) 342-6163
Fax: (336) 342-0583
Reservations:
summit.center@ncmail.net

LOCATION	Rockingham County
SIZE	336 acres
GPS	36.2461, -79.7923

As you descend the steps down the slopes of Hemlock Bluffs and catch a whiff of galax and see mammoth hemlock trees looming overhead, you may feel like you are not in Cary anymore. These eighty-foot-high north-facing slopes maintain a cool, moist microclimate that sustains a stand of eastern hemlocks about 200 miles east of its normal range in the Appalachian Mountains.

The State leases Hemlock Bluffs State Natural Area to the Town of Cary. The town owns the adjacent 50-acre Hemlock Bluffs Nature Preserve, which contains approximately three miles of interconnected trails. The Swift Creek Loop Trail offers lovely views of the bluffs and hemlocks and then descends into a floodplain along the creek. The stream is home to a surprising amount of wildlife, including muskrat and beaver. Local birders have compiled a bird list of more than 130 species for the preserve. Migratory birds that nest here include wood thrush, ovenbird, and summer tanager. In the springtime you can enjoy the floodplain's lush carpet of trilliums, mayapples and jack-in-the pulpit.

CONTACT INFO

Stevens Nature Center at
Hemlock Bluffs Preserve
2616 Kildaire Farm Road
Cary, NC 27518
Phone: 919-387-5980
Website:
www.hemlockbluffs.org

Nearby

- Falls Lake State Recreation Area: See page 38.
- Jordan Lake State Recreation Area: See page 44.
- William B. Umstead State Park: See page 64.
- Swift Creek Bluffs Nature Preserve: www.tlc-nc.org/lands/tlc/swift_creek_np.shtml
- White Pines Preserve: www.tlc-nc.org/lands/tlc/white_pines_np.shtml

LOCATION	One mile south of intersection of Tryon and Kildaire Farm roads in Cary, Wake County.
SIZE	92 acres
GPS	35.7245, -78.7863

JORDAN LAKE STATE RECREATION AREA

Jordan Lake is a reservoir located in one of the fastest growing areas of the state, with Chapel Hill, Durham, Cary, and Raleigh all nearby. It was completed in 1974, after the U.S. Army Corps of Engineers dammed the Haw River. The historic forests, farms, and whitewater stretches of the Haw and New Hope Rivers now lie beneath the reservoir; but the recreation area provides open space and natural areas for people and wildlife. Jordan Lake's seven recreation areas (Crosswinds Campground, Ebenezer, New Hope Overlook, Parkers Creek, Robeson Creek, Seaforth, Vista Point) provide a full range of recreational facilities. All are accessible by car and have boat ramps, and most have trails, swimming areas, and restroom facilities. Check the park Web site for details.

Although at times motorboat and Jet Ski traffic can deter folks who are looking for quieter pursuits, Jordan Lake has something to offer those recreationists as well. Its various habitats, including pine-hardwood forest and old fields, are home to interesting Piedmont animals and plants. The recreation area continues to add new hiking trails, including the New Hope Overlook Trail, a 5.4-mile moderate hike through upland hardwoods.

CONTACT INFO
280 State Park Road
Apex, NC 27523
Phone: (919) 362-0586
Fax: (919) 362-1621
E-mail:
jordan.lake@ncmail.net

LOCATION   Jordan Lake State Recreation Area is located in Chatham County, 21 miles southwest of Raleigh off US 64, and can be reached via NC 751 or US 15-501 from Durham and Chapel Hill. The park office is just before the bridge over Jordan Lake.

SIZE   3,916 acres of woodlands and 14,000 acres of lake

GPS   35.6748, -79.0519

Canoeists and kayakers enjoy paddling in the fingers of the lake (rather than the rougher open water with the motor craft). The Parkers Creek recreation area is a great place to kayak because there is no motorboat access, and the boat launch is a short walk from the parking lot. Triangle-area birders keep an eye on Jordan Lake because this large body of water sometimes attracts unusual birds. Birding the trails around the lake, particularly the three-mile Vista Point Trail, is a good way to see land and water birds. April through June is the best time of year to see bald eagles.

Staying Alive

Swim only in designated areas of the park, and note that there are no lifeguards on duty in these areas. Winds can whip up large waves on Jordan Lake. If you are boating, wear an approved flotation device.

Nearby

- Eno River State Park: See page 34.
- Falls Lake State Recreation Area: See page 38.
- William B. Umstead State Park: See page 64.
- Jordan Game Lands: www.ncwildlife.org
- Jordan Lake Educational State Forest: www.ncesf.org/JLESF/jlesf_about.htm

KERR LAKE STATE RECREATION AREA

One of the most heavily visited parks or recreation areas in North Carolina, Kerr Lake is a vast reservoir in the Roanoke River Valley on the North Carolina–Virginia border that was completed by the U.S. Army Corps of Engineers in 1952. While the reservoir's principal purpose is power generation, it is heavily used for recreation. Eight separate access areas provide a variety of amenities including trails, a fishing pier at the Bullocksville access area, and community buildings at four locations (check the park Web site for details). All the areas except Satterwhite Point provide boat ramps and camping for individual tents and RVs, with RV hookups. Henderson, Hibernia, and Satterwhite Point provide for group camping. Picnic facilities are available at all sites except the J. C. Cooper Campground.

If you enjoy boating, sailing, and swimming, this is a great inland freshwater destination. Motorboats and sailboats are the preferred methods of travel on the lake. The lake and its environs are home to typical Piedmont wildlife, and you should keep an eye out for wary types like river otters and raptors. In the winter, the lake can be a good spot to look for waterfowl.

CONTACT INFO

6254 Satterwhite Point Road
Henderson, NC 27537
Phone: (252) 438-7791
Fax: (252) 438-7582
E-mail: kerr.lake@ncmail.net

LOCATION   Kerr Lake State Recreation Area straddles the Vance and Warren county line north of Henderson, near the North Carolina–Virginia border; it can be reached via US 1, NC 39, or I-85. Follow the brown direction signs to the individual recreation areas. The park office is at the Satterwhite Point access area.

SIZE   3,002 acres of land, 50,000 acres of lake

GPS   36.4871, -78.3294

Staying Alive

Swim only in designated areas; there are no lifeguards at this lake. Kerr Lake can develop large waves during high wind. If you boat on the lake, you must wear an approved flotation device.

Nearby

- Kerr Lake: U.S. Army Corps of Engineers access areas and campgrounds, www.saw.usace.army.mil/jhkerr/maps.htm
- Falls Lake State Recreation Area: See page 38.
- Medoc Mountain State Park: See page 54.
- Virginia State Parks: Occoneechee and Staunton River, www.dcr.virginia.gov/state_parks/

Lake Norman is the largest constructed reservoir in North Carolina, with more than 520 miles of shoreline. Duke Energy created the reservoir by damming the Catawba River as part of a series of dams constructed to supply energy to the growing Charlotte area. (See Lake James State Park, page 18.) The park is primarily used for boating and fishing; visitors can rent pedal boats and canoes in the summer.

The park also offers unique opportunities for hiking, mountain biking, swimming, and birding. Hikers can enjoy the winding five-mile Lakeshore Trail, which offers good vistas of the lake. The Itusi Mountain Bike Trail grew to 13 miles of single-track in the spring of 2007 with the completion of the Monbo Loop Trail. Volunteers built and maintain the trail, and mountain bike Web sites and blogs rave about its design. There is a fishing pier and a swimming area with a sand beach in the south part of the park at the end of State Park Road.

From late summer through early spring, the park is a good birding spot, especially for observing wading birds. Two bridges on the

CONTACT INFO

159 Inland Sea Lane
Troutman, NC 28166
Phone: (704) 528-6350
Fax: (704) 528-5623
E-mail:
lake.norman@ncmail.net

LOCATION   The park lies at the northeast end of Lake Norman, in Iredell County, about 10 miles south of Statesville and 32 miles north of Charlotte. The park office is on State Park Road, a short distance from Troutman.

SIZE   1,679 acres of land, 32,000 acres of lake

GPS   35.6652, -80.9421

main park road are good vantage points to see egrets and herons, and migratory waterfowl can be seen here during spring and fall. Hurricane Hugo blew through in 1989, leaving lots of snags in the park that attract many species of woodpeckers.

Staying Alive

Because of underwater hazards and irregular water depths, swimming from the park shoreline is not recommended.

Nearby

· Crowders Mountain State Park: See page 30.
· South Mountains State Park: See page 62.

LOWER HAW RIVER STATE NATURAL AREA

[PARK IN PROGRESS]

The stretch of the Haw River between Bynum and the US 64 bridge has always attracted adventurous canoeists and kayakers, as this rocky stretch offers challenging rapids through a boulderfield. Anglers are also fond of this stretch of river, as evidenced by the network of fishing trails on the property. Duke University once owned this forested corridor on both sides of the river as part of Duke Forest. When university officials determined that researchers were not utilizing this section of the teaching and research forest, they decided to sell the tract. Fortunately, the N.C. Department of Environment and Natural Resources teamed up with Triangle Land Conservancy to negotiate the conservation of this property and in 2003, the State purchased the property from Duke.

The N.C. Division of Parks and Recreation is still developing its management plans for the natural area so at the moment a primitive hiking trail that hugs the river is the best way to explore the property. The 2-mile trail leads to Bynum, making for a nice 4-mile roundtrip hike.

The trailhead is located at a gravel parking area on the southern

LOCATION	Chatham County
SIZE	1,022 acres
GPS	35.7490, -79.1369

side of the US 64 bridge over the Haw. From there the trail passes beneath the highway and heads north along the eastern bank of the river. The trail climbs over steep slopes and rock outcrops and passes through wide bottomland areas with extensive beds of horsetail, a primitive plant that is rare in Chatham County. The bottomland forests contain trees such as green ash and swamp chestnut oak, and swampy depressions harbor wetland plants such as buttonbush and lizard's tail. In the spring a rare ephemeral flower – buttercup phacelia – blooms here by the thousands. Mountain laurel grows on the slopes, along with beech and red oak.

The maturity of these forests is reflected in the birdlife: 50 species of breeding birds have been recorded here, including 15 species of warblers. Prothonotary and yellow-throated warblers and northern parula all nest here. As well, wild turkey, barred owl, and pileated woodpecker find a home here.

Note that the trail is rocky in places and requires crossing a few streams, including Pokeberry Creek, which is roughly 15 yards wide.

Nearby
- Falls Lake State Recreation Area: See page 38.
- William B. Umstead State Park: See page 64.
- Jordan Game Lands: www.ncwildlife.org
- Jordan Lake Educational State Forest: www.ncesf.org/JLESF

MAYO RIVER STATE PARK

[PARK IN PROGRESS]

Along with Chimney Rock, Mayo River State Park is the "park in progress" that is closest to opening to the public with its facilities in place. As early as 2008, the State could open interim facilities at the site of the Old Mayo Park that will include picnic grounds and trails. A river-based park, the new state park will eventually provide access to a rocky Piedmont stream that attracts experienced whitewater paddlers and beginners alike. The park will encompass an approximately 12-mile stretch of the river extending from the Virginia/North Carolina border to just north of the town of Mayodan. The northern section of the river is wilder, flowing through a gorge that offers class II and III rapids, while the lower section of the river goes through a smoother section that appeals to less experienced paddlers.

This park was identified as one of 47 New Parks for a New Century. Stay tuned to the state parks Web site for news about the development of this park.

Nearby
· Hanging Rock State Park: See page 40.

LOCATION	Rockingham County
SIZE	1,967 acres
GPS	36.4643, -79.9480

MEDOC MOUNTAIN STATE PARK

Tranquil Medoc Mountain is a natural oasis in a rural setting. The park's name deserves an explanation. This "mountain" reaches a height of only 325 feet and is the eroded remnant of a larger mountain range. Former landowner Sidney Weller established a vineyard here and named the mountain Medoc in reference to the wine-growing region in France.

The park's various habitats include old fields that are converting to forest, and floodplain and hardwood forests bordering Little Fishing Creek. The park is best explored by paddling the creek's peaceful waters or by hiking on one of interconnected trails. The Bluff Loop, Discovery Loop, and Summit Loop Trails pass through floodplain forests where beeches and mountain laurel line the waterway. Uncommon this far east, the mountain laurel blooms in May and early June.

The park's open fields, successional woodlands, and swampy areas are home to a diversity of birdlife, including waterbirds such as wood duck, which breeds here, and fish-eaters like green heron and belted kingfisher. During the spring and summer, migratory

CONTACT INFO

1541 Medoc State Park Road
Hollister, NC 27844
Phone: (252) 586-6588
Fax: (252) 586-1266
E-mail:
medoc.mountain@ncmail.net

LOCATION   Medoc Mountain State Park is located in Halifax County, about nine miles off I-95 and 23 miles north of Rocky Mount. Bounded on the north by NC 561 and on the south by SR 1322, it is easily reached from the major cities of the North Carolina piedmont.

SIZE   2,385 acres

GPS   36.2570 -77.8824

songbirds like hooded and Kentucky warblers and scarlet tanager zip around the floodplain forest. American woodcocks call and display in cut-over areas in the park from about mid-January through April or May. The park is also home to a growing wild turkey population. If you sit on one of the creekside benches you may spot a river otter or muskrat swimming in the creek.

Paddlers will enjoy exploring the 2.5 miles of Little Fishing Creek that wind through the park. This section of the creek is generally shallow and slow-moving, with just a few riffles and rocks, so beginning canoeists or kayakers will enjoy the experience. Organizing a shuttle enables paddlers to take a pleasant 1.5- to 2-hour paddle by putting in at the bridge on Medoc State Park Road (SR 1322), which has a gravel parking area and steps leading to a put-in. Take out at a bridge on Medoc Mountain Road (SR 1002), where there is a grass parking area. The creek is a popular fishing spot, boasting bluegill, largemouth bass, and redbreast sunfish.

The park is due to expand when The Nature Conservancy transfers 1,507 acres to the park; the property was previously owned by International Paper Corporation.

Staying Alive
Take proper precautions when hiking in the spring and summer to avoid tick bites. Paddlers should check with the park staff before embarking on a trip to find out about current water conditions, and wear personal flotation devices on the water.

Nearby
· Roanoke Canal Trail: www.roanokecanal.com
· Roanoke River Paddle Trail: www.roanokeriverpartners.org

MORROW MOUNTAIN STATE PARK

Along the Yadkin and Pee Dee river system, one of the oldest mountain ranges in the eastern United States towers above the surrounding piedmont landscape. These are the Uwharrie Mountains, and they began forming some 500 million years ago, a testament to the unremitting power of erosion. Morrow is the tallest of the range's four major peaks and measures 936 feet.

Morrow Mountain State Park borders Lake Tillery, where the Yadkin and Pee Dee Rivers are impounded, and is one of the more diverse parks in the state, offering hiking, camping, horseback riding, swimming, boating, and significant cultural and natural history all in one park. Ten thousand or more years ago, Native Americans were already in the Uwharries; in the 18th century, explorers encountered Sapano, Saura, and Catawba tribes in the region. The park contains a number of quarry sites where Native Americans gathered rhyolite to make chipped-stone tools.

The park's 15 miles of trails provide pathways for solitary explorations of the Uwharrie landscape and range from easy to strenuous in difficulty. The 4.1-mile Fall Mountain Trail is the

CONTACT INFO

49104 Morrow
Mountain Road
Albemarle, NC 28001
Phone: (704) 982-4402
Fax: (704) 982-5323
E-mail: morrow.mountain@
ncmail.net

LOCATION The park is located six miles east of Albemarle, in Stanley County, and is accessible from NC 24/27, NC 73, and NC 740.

SIZE 4,496 acres

GPS 35.3635, -80.0832

longest and most challenging in the park and takes hikers to a volcanic outcrop with a good view of the Yadkin River. The Three Rivers Trail is an easy 0.6-mile loop that goes through a marshy area and then to a cove along the Yadkin–Pee Dee. Look for frogs and wading birds in the cove along the river. One hundred and seventy bird species have been recorded in the park, and this is a good place to visit during spring migration, particularly for warblers. The park also provides 16 miles of bridle trails.

Primitive, RV, and group camping is available by permit, along with six rustic cabins, each of which accommodates up to six people with two bedrooms, a kitchen, bathroom, and a living room with a fireplace. The park has a huge swimming pool, open from June through Labor Day, with adjacent changing rooms, restrooms, and showers. A small shop offers drinks and snacks at poolside. A boat ramp, boathouse with canoe and rowboat rentals, and a fishing pier provide access to the Pee Dee River and Lake Tillery.

Staying Alive
Park gates are locked at specific times that vary with the seasons. Be sure to check the times before using the park.

Nearby
· Uwharrie National Forest: www.cs.unca.edu/nfsnc/recreation/uwharrie/

PILOT MOUNTAIN STATE PARK

Your first sight of the gray rocky massif of Pilot Mountain looming 1,400 feet above the Piedmont landscape will certainly be memorable. Like nearby Hanging Rock, this monadnock is a remnant of the ancient Sauratown Mountain range. Over millions of years, erosion weathered away softer, less-resistant rock around the pinnacle, leaving a rocky knob circled by a collar of green vegetation. The popular mountain section features the knob itself and most of the park's facilities.

CONTACT INFO

1792 Pilot Knob Park Road
Pinnacle, NC 27043
Phone: (336) 325-2355
Fax: (336) 325-2751
E-mail:
pilot.mountain@ncmail.net

The park offers more than 24 miles of hiking trails, including 10.5 miles that are also open to horses. If you hike the trails in springtime, you will see mountain laurel, galax, and rhododendron in bloom. Although you cannot hike to Big Pinnacle, the summit of Pilot Mountain, you need only hike the 0.1-mile trail to the Little Pinnacle Overlook for an unobstructed view of the peak. The 0.8-mile Jomeokee Trail circles the base of Big Pinnacle and gives you the best view of the rocky cliffs and rock ledges where birds forage for food and lizards skitter into crevices. Ambitious hikers will be interested in the 21-mile Sauratown Trail, which is part of the Mountains to Sea Trail and connects

LOCATION   Pilot Mountain straddles the line between two counties, Surry and Yadkin, 24 miles north of Winston-Salem and 14 miles south of Mount Airy. The park is divided into three sections: the mountain section, off US 52; a northern river section 10 miles away, also off US 52; and a southern river section 20 miles away, off NC 67. The park office is in the mountain section of the park.

SIZE   3,703 acres

GPS   36.3410, -80.4775

Hanging Rock and Pilot Mountain State Parks. Visit www.sauratowntrails.org for more information. Rock climbing and rappelling are allowed in designated sections of the park, but please visit the park Web site for more information.

Birders enjoy visiting the park in the fall to view migrating raptors. Thirteen different species have been observed from the Little Pinnacle Overlook, broad-winged hawk being the most abundant, along with sharp-shinned and Cooper's hawks.

To drive to the northern river section you have to ford Horne Creek three times, so you should contact the park office first to check on current water conditions. A two-mile section of the 165-mile Yadkin River Canoe Trail passes through this part of the park and is particularly lovely, with river birches and sycamores leaning over the waterway. This section of the river is typically shallow and broad, and at certain times it is possible to wade over to the Yadkin Islands in the middle of the river. The larger of the two islands has two canoe campsites. Note that you cannot rent canoes at the park.

Staying Alive
Exercise caution any time you are hiking in areas with lots of rocks and potential drops. Paddlers should contact the park office for more information about river conditions.

Nearby
· Hanging Rock State Park: See page 40.

RAVEN ROCK STATE PARK

At Raven Rock, the Cape Fear River courses over the Fall Line, where the harder rocks of the Piedmont give way to the softer sediments of the coastal plain. This outcropping spans more than a mile across the river. Ravens once roosted on the ledges of this rock that historically served as a landmark for river traffic.

Most of the visitor facilities and 11 miles of hiking trails are located in the more rugged southern section of the park. The 2.6-mile Raven Rock loop goes to the famed rock itself, and a stairway leads to the bottom of this massive rock overhang. The 0.6-mile (one-way) Fish Traps Trail leads to a rock outcrop where Native Americans fished with baskets below the rocks. The more challenging 5-mile Campbell Creek Loop is less traveled than other trails but passes through some of the prettiest scenery in the park. The trail hugs the banks of Campbell Creek part of the way and winds through slopes covered in mountain laurel thickets. A short spur, the Lanier Falls Trail, leads to another scenic rock outcrop on the river. The park's northern section offers 7 miles of bridle trails.

CONTACT INFO

3009 Raven Rock Road
Lillington, NC 27546
Phone: (910) 893-4888
Fax: (910) 814-2200
E-mail:
info.ravenrock@ncmail.net

LOCATION Raven Rock State Park is in Harnett County, nine miles west of Lillington and 20 miles east of Sanford on US 421.

SIZE 4,667 acres

GPS 35.4728, -78.9057

Raven Rock's floodplain forests harbor large sycamore and beech trees and a wealth of early spring wildflowers including bloodroot, Solomon's seal, and Dutchman's breeches. Anglers will want to test the waters for largemouth bass and bluegill. The park's many small streams and tributaries are home to salamanders, frogs, and toads, making this a great destination for a frog-and-toad-listening expedition in late winter and early spring. After a rain, you will likely hear many tree frogs calling.

With 183 bird species identified at the park, birders enjoy hiking through the diverse habitats. Look for warblers in the spring and fall, raptors throughout the year, and water and wading birds along the river and tributaries.

The 56-mile Cape Fear Canoe Trail, which begins at the access point on the US 1 bridge on the Deep River, runs through the park. A canoe-in campsite offers six sites and is located 1.7 miles from the park office. Call the park office to reserve a campsite.

Staying Alive
Hikers should be cautious when walking on slopes and rocks along the river's edge, particularly after a rain. Canoeists and kayakers should exercise their normal caution, checking water levels and conditions and wearing flotation devices while on the water.

Nearby
· Jordan Lake State Recreation Area: See page 44.
· Weymouth Woods Sandhills Nature Preserve: See page 110.

SOUTH MOUNTAINS STATE PARK

The South Mountains range is the largest unfragmented wilderness area in North Carolina's piedmont. An outlier of the Blue Ridge range, these mountains are not as tall as the Blue Ridge range, but they are steep and rugged. The state park and adjacent South Mountains Game Lands protect a 37,000-acre forested corridor for wide-ranging animals like black bear, bobcat, and neotropical migratory songbirds.

The park is home to seldom seen mammals such as mink, as well as reptiles and amphibians, including unique salamander species and numerous snakes – mostly harmless species, but also the venomous timber rattlesnake and copperhead. The birdlife tends to be representative of the piedmont, but on the list of 66 species that nest here you will find species normally associated with the mountains, such as ruffed grouse and rose-breasted grosbeak. Rainbow, brook, and brown trout swim in the pristine streams. In springtime the slopes come alive with blooming mountain laurel and rhododendron, as well as wildflowers like jack-in-the-pulpit and lady's slipper.

CONTACT INFO

3001 South Mountains State
Park Avenue
Connelly Springs, NC 28612
Phone: (828) 433-4772
Fax: (828) 433-4778
E-mail:
south.mountains@ncmail.net

LOCATION   South Mountains State Park is located off SR 1901, 18 miles south of Morganton in Burke County, and is easily accessible from I-40.

SIZE   17,448 acres

GPS   35.6001, -81.6425

Hiking into the park's interior can be a real wilderness experience. Forty miles of hiking trails, primarily moderate to strenuous, lead to camping areas and peaks rising to 3,000 feet. The most popular trails are the strenuous 1.2-mile High Shoals Falls Loop and the 2.0-mile hike to Chestnut Knob Overlook. Chestnut oak, oak-hickory, and cove forests support more than 800 species of plants, 100 of which are designated as federal or state rare species. The boulder-strewn creeks that run through the park drain into the Catawba River watershed and have carved steep slopes over time. In places the water tumbles over rocks in spectacular waterfalls, such as High Shoals Falls on the Jacob's Fork River, which plunges 80 feet over a bare rock face. The park's facilities include a 37-stall horse barn and 29 miles of equestrian trails. Mountain bikers love the strenuous 18-mile mountain bike loop.

Staying Alive

Even park superintendents have been bitten by venomous snakes at South Mountains, so staying on the trails is a good idea. Be careful around cliff faces and waterfalls.

Nearby

- South Mountains Game Land, managed by the N.C. Wildlife Resources Commission, is adjacent to the park. Like other game lands in the state, the area is open for hunting, fishing, and hiking. For more information, see www.ncwildlife.org.
- Crowders Mountain State Park: See page 30.
- Lake Norman State Park: See page 48.

WILLIAM B. UMSTEAD STATE PARK

Flying into Raleigh-Durham Airport, northwest of Raleigh, you see the expansive forested island of William B. Umstead State Park surrounded by highways and development. Located within one of the country's fastest growing urban centers, the park has become a natural recreation center and refuge for thousands of locals in Durham, Chapel Hill, and Raleigh, and for people who visit the area from around the globe.

The park's landscape reflects a typical story of land use in North Carolina's piedmont, where farming practices eventually depleted and eroded topsoil until farming became unproductive. In 1935, during the Great Depression, the Resettlement Administration purchased the property for a demonstration project, and the property was deeded to the state for a park in 1943.

Today, the park offers something for all types of outdoor enthusiasts. The amenities have not supplanted the park's wild qualities, fortunately, as the property has been transformed from marginal farmland to a peaceful piedmont natural area with its associated wildlife, such as gray fox and wild turkey.

CONTACT INFO

8801 Glenwood Avenue
Raleigh, NC 27617
Phone: (919) 571-4170
Fax: (919) 571-4161
E-mail:
william.umstead@ncmail.net

LOCATION The park lies between Raleigh and Durham, in Wake County. The Crabtree Creek section, which includes the visitor center and camping facilities, is located 10 miles northwest of Raleigh off US 70. The entrance to the Reedy Creek section is 11 miles west of Raleigh off I-40, on Harrison Avenue.

SIZE 5,598 acres

GPS 35.8476, -78.7469

Twenty miles of easy to moderate trails showcase various habitats, from mixed pine and hardwood forests to rocky piedmont streams. The 4.5-mile Company Mill loop in the Reedy Creek section is a wonderful introduction to the park, as it runs along Crabtree Creek and by the remains of the Company Mill dam, once one of the largest gristmills in the area. Umstead also contains 13 miles of shared bridle and mountain bike trails.

Visitors can rent canoes and rowboats and fish at three manmade lakes, which include the 55-acre Big Lake. Swimming is available at Sycamore and Reedy Creek Lakes for registered group campers only. Extensive facilities are available for group activities, including dining facilities and cabins, and numerous picnic areas. The park offers tent and trailer camping in developed group areas and two primitive campgrounds.

Drop by the visitor center to learn more about the park's transformation to an urban oasis. A piedmont forest is a great place to learn about the recovery of natural communities and the challenges of land stewardship in an area facing pressure from a growing population.

Staying Alive
You can get lost at Umstead. If you're not familiar with the park, pick up a trail map at the visitor center, or download one from the park Web site.

Nearby
- Eno River State Park: See page 34.
- Falls Lake State Recreation Area: See page 38.
- Jordan Lake State Recreation Area: See page 44.
- Duke Forest: www.dukeforest.duke.edu

coastal plain

Carvers Creek Sandhills State Park

CAROLINA BEACH STATE PARK

Carolina Beach State Park has wide appeal among boaters, birders, anglers, and plant-lovers. The park is located on the northwest, inland side of the barrier island of Carolina Beach. This section of New Hanover County became an island in 1928, when the dredging of the Intracoastal Waterway created a channel called Snow's Cut that connects Masonboro Sound to the Cape Fear River.

More than six miles of hiking trails and boardwalks meander through longleaf pine forests mixed with turkey oaks, pocosin, and brackish marsh bordering the Cape Fear River. The .5-mile Flytrap Trail gives hikers a glimpse of some of the five species of carnivorous plants found in the park, including the Venus flytrap. The three-mile Sugarloaf Trail is named for a 50-foot-high dune that has served as a navigational landmark for boats on the Cape Fear since the 1700s. The trail passes by a variety of habitats, including three unusual rain-fed depressions: Cypress Pond, which is covered by a bonsai-like cypress forest; the aptly named Lily Pond; and Grass Pond, which supports sundews and butterworts on its fringes. These fish-free wetlands are home to a diverse frog population and are worth a visit after a good rain.

CONTACT INFO
1010 State Park Road
Carolina Beach, NC 28428
Phone: (910) 458-8206
Fax: (910) 458-7770
E-mail:
carolina.beach@ncmail.net

LOCATION	Ten miles south of Wilmington, in New Hanover County, off NC 421.
SIZE	420 acres
GPS	34.0467, -77.9098

Sandwiched between Snow's Cut and the Cape Fear, the park's marina offers motorboats and kayaks access to the Atlantic Ocean, the estuarine waters of Masonboro Sound, and the Cape Fear. Anglers have a wealth of choices both offshore and onshore, including fishing from a wheelchair-accessible deck or from the river banks. The potential catch includes striped bass, flounder, and spot.

Birders hoping to see a showy painted bunting have a good chance at the park during its breeding season from about mid-April through July. This multicolored finch inhabits shrub thickets on the forest edge, such as those found along the Sugarloaf Trail. Check the feeder near the marina as well. The species is declining due to habitat loss, as well as a caged-bird trade in its wintering grounds in Latin America. If you want to make a weekend of your trip to the state park, the 83-site campground tucked inside a live oak grove is a tranquil spot.

Staying Alive
Boaters should follow standard boating safety and check the weather report before heading out from the marina. Hikers should be aware of summer-month hazards such as biting insects. Sunscreen is always a good idea at the coast.

Nearby
· Fort Fisher State Recreation Area: See page 80.

CARVERS CREEK SANDHILLS STATE PARK

[PARK IN PROGRESS]

The ongoing conservation work in the Sandhills region got a real boost in 2005, when the N.C. Legislature authorized the creation of Carvers Creek Sandhills State Park, the first state park in Cumberland County. The core of the new park is the 1,393-acre Carvers Creek tract. This former Nature Conservancy holding just north of Fayetteville contains a significant remnant of the storied longleaf pine landscape. Thanks to the Conservancy's active prescribed burning program, the property's longleaf forests are thriving. Carvers Creek winds through the natural area and the property's wetland habitats, including seeps and streamhead pocosins, are home to a unique mix of plants and animals.

The spring of 2007 brought more exciting developments for the new state park, when The Nature Conservancy announced that it would donate 1,380-acre Long Valley Farm to the State. Located in Spring Lake just a few miles from Carvers Creek, Long Valley Farm is a mixture of forest and farmland, with about two-thirds of the property containing longleaf pine woodlands, a cypress-gum swamp, and wet meadows with pitcher plants. Jumping Run Creek, a tributary of the Little River, flows through the property.

LOCATION	Cumberland County
SIZE	1,393 acres
GPS	35.1814, -78.8879

Initial biological inventories report that the property is home to some rare creatures, including the federally listed red-cockaded woodpecker and the loggerhead shrike. Fort Bragg surrounds the farm, so the new state park is a key piece in the corridor of connected lands that support healthy Sandhills habitats.

Long Valley Farm was once a retreat for the Rockefeller family. When owner James Stillman Rockefeller died in 2004 at the age of 102, he bequeathed the property to The Nature Conservancy to ensure that it would be protected from development. The property contains a 100-acre lake and a rambling old house and is listed on the National Register of Historic Places.

The Division of Parks and Recreation is still developing management plans for the new state park, so stay tuned for further developments.

Nearby
· Weymouth Woods Sandhills Nature Preserve: See page 110.

CHOWAN SWAMP STATE NATURAL AREA

Ⅰf you are looking for a tranquil paddling destination, head for the Chowan River in northeastern North Carolina. The Chowan Swamp State Natural Area protects a large swath of the northern shore of the river and averages about 3 miles in width. The N.C. Wildlife Resources Commission and Forestry Foundation of North Carolina manage other sections of the river and floodplain.

Chowan Swamp contains a bottomland hardwood forest with old bald cypress and water tupelo. Small ridges or "islands" support upland forests with beeches and oaks. The river's blackwater tributaries - Bennett's, Catherine, and Sarem Creeks - are well-worth a detour off the main river. As you glide into the placid backwaters you will paddle through freshwater marshes that contain prairie cordgrass and wild rice. The river and creek habitats are home to river otter, bobcat, black bear, and mink. Migratory songbirds typical of swamp habitats nest here, including prothonotary and Swainson's warblers.

The Chowan is part of the Albemarle Regional Canoe/Kayak Paddling Trail. The nonprofit Roanoke River Partners manages

LOCATION	Gates County
SIZE	6,066 acres
GPS	36.3698, -76.7726

five camping platforms on Holladay Island in the middle of the Chowan, downstream from the blackwater tributary streams described above. The platforms are located approximately 20 miles from Edenton and are accessible only by boat. Each raised platform can hold as many as eight campers and their tents. A N.C. Wildlife Resources Commission boat ramp is located one mile from the island and is used for launching motorboats. You can launch canoes or kayaks from the Cannon's Ferry Heritage River Walk located at Cannon Ferry, on the eastern shore of the Chowan, off of Highway 32 in Chowan County. For more information about the platforms, visit www.roanokeriverpartners.org/RiverCamping_HolladayIsland.htm.

Nearby
· Dismal Swamp State Park: See page 76.
· Merchants Millpond State Park: See page 104.

With towns and farms crowding in from all sides, Cliffs of the Neuse is a small green refuge along the Neuse River. For 600 yards along the river's south bank, cliffs rise 90 feet, exposing the area's geological history and providing a unique vista of the river and surrounding forest.

The park's diverse habitats support plants that one might find in the mountains, such as galax and Virginia pine, as well as species more typical of the coastal plain, such as Spanish moss, which you see draped over cypress and oak trees. This epiphyte is in the pineapple family and absorbs nutrients from rainwater and dew. Floodplain forests along the river contain cypress and river birch.

You can explore the park's habitats on four easy trails, each half a mile or less in length. A short trail leads across Mill Creek, the historic site of a gristmill that ground cornmeal and connects to trails that pass by Still Creek, where whiskey stills once produced moonshine. Hiking along the Neuse in the springtime you can see flowering dogwood, hollies, and jasmine. You may also see some of the migratory birds that nest here in the spring and summer,

CONTACT INFO

345-A Park Entrance Road
Seven Springs, NC 28578
Phone: (919) 778-6234
Fax: (919) 778-7447
E-mail:
cliffs.neuse@ncmail.net

LOCATION	The state park is in Wayne County, 14 miles southeast of Goldsboro, on NC 111.
SIZE	892 acres
GPS	35.2357, -77.8854

including prothonotary warbler and northern parula, which nests in Spanish moss. Look for waterbirds along the river such as kingfisher, herons, and wood duck.

Park visitors can swim in an 11-acre spring-fed lake with a sandy beach and fish in the river, which is home to bluegill, largemouth bass, and catfish.

Seven Springs is a short paddle downriver. Formerly known as Whitehall, it was a holiday mecca at the turn of the 20th century where people drank "curative mineral waters" and rode riverboats upstream to see the cliffs.

In 2007, the Neuse was listed by American Rivers as one of America's 10 most endangered rivers, and the park offers a quiet and beautiful place to reflect on the river's past, and to be hopeful about its future. For information on the health of the river and to learn what you can do to make a difference, contact the Neuse River Foundation at www.neuseriver.org and American Rivers at www.americanrivers.org.

Staying Alive
Be careful near the river and around high bluffs. Carefully consider the water quality before taking a dip.

Nearby
· Howell Woods: www.johnstoncc.edu/howellwoods/

DISMAL SWAMP STATE PARK

Before European settlement, the Great Dismal Swamp may have encompassed more than one million acres between the present-day James River in Virginia and the Albemarle Sound in North Carolina. This low-lying basin was covered in a mosaic of bald cypress, swamp black gum, and tupelo gum, with scattered Atlantic white cedar forests and pocosins.

When enterprising European explorers, including George Washington, began to investigate the edges of the swamp, they sensed profits. Beginning in the 1760s, a succession of businesses dug canals to drain the wetland and logged cypress and Atlantic white cedar to produce shingles and other building materials. Today, every acre in the swamp has been logged at least once. But all was not lost. In the 1970s, timber companies donated more than 59,000 acres of the swamp to form Dismal Swamp National Wildlife Refuge and the Dismal Swamp State Natural Area (now State Park).

The Dismal Swamp's colorful human history begins with Native Americans who camped on high ground and hunted waterfowl

CONTACT INFO

2294 US Highway 17 North
South Mills, NC 27938
Phone: (252) 771-6593
Fax: (252) 771-9944
E-mail:
dismal.swamp@ncmail.net

LOCATION The park is located in Camden County and extends west of US 17, just south of the Virginia–North Carolina state line.

SIZE 14,344 acres

GPS 36.5155, -76.3799

with bolas some 9,000 years ago. When European settlers began logging the swamp, they forced enslaved Africans to undertake this brutal work. Archaeologists have uncovered evidence of maroon colonies in the Dismal. These groups of fugitive African American slaves hid in camps in the swamp as they traveled to freedom on the Underground Railroad.

Although the Dismal is not the "howling wilderness" of yesterday, it is still a critical wildlife habitat. The national wildlife refuge and state park provide more than 22 square miles of unbroken forest for abundant wildlife, including black bear and bobcat. At least 62 bird species nest here, and half of these species are neotropical migrants.

As this book went to press, the park was in the process of completing a visitor's center that will be accessible from a floating bridge across the Dismal Swamp Canal. Projected to open to the public in early 2008, the park will offer approximately 20 miles of hiking trails and 17 miles of mountain biking trails. Boardwalks will penetrate the swamp and parallel the storied Dismal Swamp Canal. Check the state park Web site for the latest information on these developments.

Staying Alive
Visiting the Dismal Swamp in the summer can be pretty, well, dismal, because of the abundant mosquitoes, deerflies, and ticks. Determined visitors should arm themselves with long-sleeved shirts and pants, insect repellent, and hats.

Nearby
· Dismal Swamp National Wildlife Refuge: See www.fws.gov/northeast/greatdismalswamp/.
· Merchants Millpond State Park: See page 104.

Dismal Swamp NWR

How dismal is it?

History and literature are replete with negative references to the Great Dismal Swamp, the first being attributed to map maker August Herrman, who wrote in 1670 that the area was "for the most parts Low Suncken Swampy Land not well passable but with great difficulty and therein harbours Tygers Bears and other Devouringe Creatures." The myth was perpetuated with William Byrd's *Histories of the Dividing Line betwixt Virginia and North Carolina*, in which he described his hapless band of surveyors getting mired and lost in the great morass, concluding that "the Eternal Shade that broods over this mighty Bog, and hinders the sunbeams from blessing the Ground, makes it an uncomfortable habitation for any thing that has life."

For a more current and affectionate tribute to the swamp, read *The Great Dismal* by Bland Simpson.

Fort Fisher State Recreation Area protects a unique feature on the southeast coast: a beach that is free of houses and condos. For a small fee you can drive a four-wheel-drive vehicle onto the beach at specified times designated to protect people and wildlife. Better yet, you can hike down the beach or along the Basin Trail and boardwalk and enjoy exploring the area on foot.

As Duke University geologist and beach expert Orrin Pilkey has explained, sandy beaches move around, and with successive trips to the area, you will notice that the beachfront changes continually as winds and currents shift. As you enter the park, you drive through a remnant maritime forest of live oaks and hollies, but the vegetation becomes sparser as you travel south onto the beach. Loggerhead sea turtles nest on the beach; park staff reported 33 nests in 2006. Shorebirds, including least tern, black skimmer, and possibly the federally endangered piping plover, also nest here. When you visit, please stay out of roped-off nesting areas.

The one-mile Basin Trail takes you over a boardwalk and through a tidal salt marsh and past the former residence of the Fort Fisher

CONTACT INFO

1000 Loggerhead Road
Kure Beach, NC 28449
Phone: (910) 458-5798
Fax: (910) 458-3722
E-mail: fort.fisher@ncmail.net

LOCATION The recreation area lies five miles south of Carolina Beach, off US 421, in New Hanover County. It can also be reached by the Southport–Fort Fisher ferry, which crosses the Cape Fear River. See the latest ferry schedule at www.ncdot.org/transit/ferry.

SIZE 287 acres

GPS 33.9534, -77.9290

The Fort Fisher Hermit

Robert Harrill was born in 1893 and spent most of his life in the North Carolina mountains. After a life of stops and starts, working in the mountains, he was committed to a state mental hospital. Looking for his true course in life, he left the mountains and hitchhiked across the state, finally taking up residence in a World War II ammunition storage at Fort Fisher. During his 17 years at Fort Fisher, Harrill became a local celebrity, offering lectures about his life and insights. He was found dead in 1972. The cause of his death is still a mystery.

Hermit (see sidebar). The trail passes through a nursery of coastal life where larval marine animals begin their lives. In October, you may see masses of migratory monarch butterflies hanging from junipers. The beach offers good swimming and surf fishing for bluefish and puppy drum. The area's diverse habitats – the beach, salt marsh, shrub thickets, maritime forest, and mudflats – offer interesting birding opportunities. During the winter, thousands of shorebirds gather on the sand flats, and you may spot merlins or peregrine falcons hunting them.

Staying Alive

Exercise caution when swimming. It is easy to get bogged down while driving on the beach, and even park staff get stuck. State-owned vehicles are not allowed to tow visitors' vehicles.

Nearby

- Carolina Beach State Park: See page 68.
- Smith Island Complex: www.ncnerr.org, www.bhic.org
- Zeke's Island Estuarine Reserve: www.ncnerr.org

FORT MACON STATE PARK

One of the most heavily visited state parks in North Carolina, Fort Macon receives approximately 1.3 million visitors every year. The park's popularity is due to its one-of-a-kind Civil War fort, its scenic recreational beach, and its location on the rapidly developing Bogue Banks. Located on the eastern end of the barrier island chain overlooking Beaufort Inlet, the park is the largest natural area remaining on the island. Sections of the park, particularly the Elliott Coues Nature Trail, which wanders through a maritime shrub thicket, have the flavor of the Bogue Banks of old.

CONTACT INFO

2300 East Fort Macon Road
Atlantic Beach, NC 28512
Phone: (252) 726-3775
Fax: (252) 726-2497
E-mail:
fort.macon@ncmail.net

The top of the fort provides a 360-degree view of the surrounding landscape, including Bogue Inlet and the Atlantic Ocean. The brick and stone five-sided fort is an impressive architectural feat. To really feel the history, visit the fort at off-peak times and wander through the maze of 26 rooms – called casements – housed behind its 4.5-foot thick brick walls. Look for the replica of a brick baking oven and the restored hot shot furnace that was used to heat cannonballs. North Carolina Confederate forces seized the fort in 1861 and occupied it for a year, bolstering the defenses with 54

LOCATION   The park extends along the eastern end of Bogue Banks in Carteret County, not far from Atlantic Beach. The fort is located at the tip of the island.

SIZE   424 acres

GPS   34.6965, -76.6907

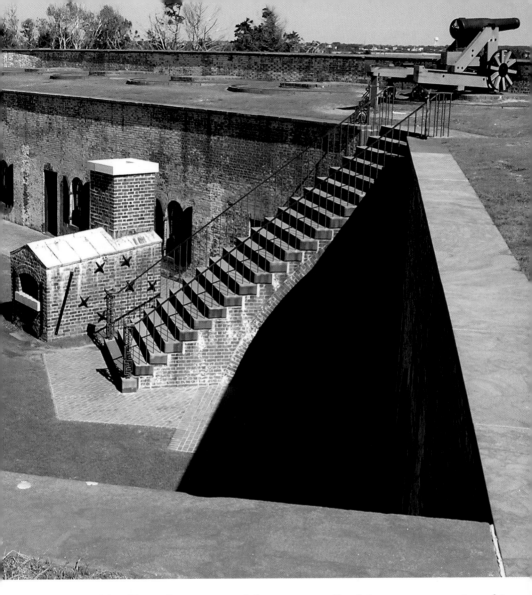

cannons. In 1862, Union forces captured the 400 some Confederate troops garrisoned in the fort and later released them as prisoners of war. The Civilian Conservation Corps restored the fort in 1934 and 1935. The park offers guided tours and exhibitions showcasing the military history of the fort that feature musket demonstrations and cannon-firing. The Friends of Fort Macon (www.clis.com/friends) is another resource for those interested in the fort and its preservation.

The park is a good spot for birding because it is surrounded by water on three sides (Atlantic Ocean, Beaufort Inlet, and Bogue Sound). On the beach you can see many typical shore and wading birds, such as terns, gulls, and migratory shorebirds at certain times of year. Painted buntings can be seen during the summer (from about mid-April through July) in thickets around the fort. Walking the Elliott Coues Nature Trail can offer rewarding looks at warblers

continued next page

during fall and spring migration, and during the breeding season, the showy orchard oriole. The top of the fort provides a good vantage point to see migrating tree swallows and hawks after cold fronts pass through the area in late September through October. The park also offers visitors a bathhouse and two picnic areas. The beach is a popular swimming area and is staffed by lifeguards from June through Labor Day.

Theodore Roosevelt State Natural Area

Theodore Roosevelt State Natural Area is located eight miles to the west of Fort Macon. Much of the 265-acre tract is not accessible to the public because of its fragile nature, but you can get a feel for Bogue Banks' only remaining intact maritime forest by walking on the two nature trails at the N.C. Aquarium at Pine Knoll Shores. The 0.5-mile Alice Hoffman Trail, which you access through the aquarium, takes you through the maritime forest and swamp forest and has a nice spur trail to East Pond, a brackish pond on the edge of salt marsh on Bogue Sound. The Theodore Roosevelt Trail begins at the southern end of the parking lot outside the aquarium. Both trails can be good for birding in the spring and fall. For more information about visiting the aquarium, go to www.ncaquariums.com.

Staying Alive

The usual coastal hazards apply at Fort Macon – be cautious while swimming, and bring your sunscreen and insect repellent during the warmer months.

Nearby

- Cedar Island National Wildlife Refuge: www.fws.gov/cedarisland
- Croatan National Forest: www.cs.unca.edu/nfsnc

Examining the birds

One of North America's renowned early ornithologists, Dr. Elliott Coues, was stationed at the fort during 1869 to 1870. Like many ornithologists, Coues supported his passion for avifauna by working as a medical doctor. Fort Macon park staff research indicates that Coues may have spent much of his time at the fort watching and collecting birds, and writing his magnum opus, *Key to North American Birds,* one of the earliest bird field guides for the country. Plans are being developed to build the Coastal Education Center at the park, which will feature exhibits focusing on coastal processes and fort history, as well as Coues's contribution to ornithology.

GOOSE CREEK STATE PARK

O n the eastern shore of the Pamlico River, Goose Creek State Park lies only 10 feet above sea level and is drained by three creeks. Goose Creek runs through the western side of the park into the Pamlico, where it is joined by Flatty Creek, while Mallard Creek drains along its eastern end. You might like to begin your visit to the park in the environmental education and visitor center, which offers interactive exhibits, a beautiful five-minute video overview of the park, and a discovery room where you can learn about life in wetlands.

Seven miles of trails wind through the park. Although the property was previously owned by Weyerhaeuser and thus contains a lot of recovering pine plantations, sections along the river are quite scenic and live oaks draped in Spanish moss provide that quintessential Southern low country feeling. Take the Flatty Creek Trail over a series of boardwalks to reach an observation deck, or meander along the Goose Creek Trail to the sandy riverbank at the Live Oak Trail. The trails take you through pines and hardwoods, scrub thickets, and swamp forest. Grasses and black needlerush grow along the brackish marsh at the shoreline of the Pamlico River.

CONTACT INFO

2190 Camp Leach Road
Washington, NC 27889
Phone: (252) 923-2191
Fax: (252) 923-0052
E-mail:
goose.creek@ncmail.net

LOCATION The park is situated off US 264, 10 miles east of Washington, in Beaufort County, on the north side of the Pamlico River.

SIZE 1,672 acres

GPS 35.4725, -76.9130

Pileated and red-bellied woodpeckers, among other species, are seen in the park all year. Springtime brings nesting warblers, including northern parula, prothonotary warbler, and common yellowthroat. You can launch a canoe at Dinah's Landing and paddle on a canoe trail northward up Goose Creek through the remains of early 20th-century logging operations. You will have to bring your own boat, and be sure to pick up a paddling guide at the visitor's center. There is a primitive campground nearby with 12 tent sites.

Staying Alive

The park's large tick population includes the lone star tick, which may carry both Rocky Mountain spotted fever and Lyme disease. Proceed with caution when walking in summer months, and use repellent, tuck in your pants and shirts, and wear light-colored clothing so ticks will be more visible.

Nearby

- Pettigrew State Park: See page 106.
- Lake Mattamuskeet National Wildlife Refuge: www.fws.gov/mattamuskeet
- Pocosin Lakes National Wildlife Refuge: www.fws.gov/pocosinlakes
- Roanoke River National Wildlife Refuge: www.fws.gov/roanokeriver
- Swanquarter National Wildlife Refuge: www.fws.gov/swanquarter

HAMMOCKS BEACH STATE PARK

If you have a limited amount of time to spend at Hammocks Beach State Park, you should poke around the exhibit hall in the visitor center, where you can learn about the dynamic habitats on North Carolina's barrier islands. A mini-theater features a film that interprets the island's importance as a nesting site for the endangered loggerhead sea turtle. Other exhibits focus on Native American history, constellations, and climate.

But if you have a day or a weekend, plan to visit Bear Island. The park's chief attraction, this unspoiled barrier island has a flawless 3.5-mile beach, and unlike most of the state's other barrier islands, it is entirely undeveloped. You can reach the island with your own motorboat or kayak, or for a small fee take the park's passenger ferry, which operates from Memorial Day through Labor Day. The ferry schedule is updated on the park Web site. Paddlers can follow a designated paddling trail to the island.

Island visitors can swim, walk, fish, or bird as they desire. A lifeguard patrols a designated swimming area during summer months. Surf fishing is particularly good during the fall. Birders

CONTACT INFO

1572 Hammocks Beach Road
Swansboro, NC 28584
Phone (park office):
(910) 326-4881;
(Bear Island): (910) 326-3553
Fax: (910) 326-2060
E-mail: hammocks.beach@
ncmail.net

LOCATION	The park, including the park office, visitor center, and ferry dock, are off NC 24, between Jacksonville and Morehead City near Swansboro, in Onslow County. Bear Island can be reached by private boat or the park ferry.
SIZE	1,138 acres
GPS	34.6335, -77.1443

can explore various habitats and look for nesting shorebirds such as black skimmers and terns, wintering flocks of shorebirds, raptors, and painted buntings in the thickets during the spring and summer. While scanning the area, keep an eye out for bottlenosed dolphins in the surf. If you can, take advantage of the rare opportunity to camp on an isolated barrier island. There are only 17 primitive and family campsites on the island, so book early.

Bear Island is a loggerhead turtle nesting beach, and each summer adult female loggerheads return to their natal beach (where they were born) to lay their eggs. Hatchlings "boil" out of the nest a couple of months later, headed for the ocean. If you are lucky enough to see them, leave them alone, as they are endangered and federally protected.

Huggins Island, east of Bear Island, contains a rare swamp forest. It is managed as a nature preserve and does not contain any trails or facilities. You can reach it only by private boat.

Staying Alive
If you paddle over to Bear Island you will cross the Intracoastal Waterway, so be wary of watercraft, tides, and wind. If swimming, watch for rip currents along the beach. There is an emergency phone for campers located at the bathhouse.

Nearby
· Fort Macon State Park and Theodore Roosevelt State Natural Area: See page 82.
· Croatan National Forest: www.cs.unca.edu/nfsnc/recreation/recreate.htm

JOCKEY'S RIDGE STATE PARK

Jockey's Ridge is a medano, an enormous hill of shifting sand that lacks vegetation. It is the tallest natural dune system in the eastern United States. Geologists believe that the dune system, which fluctuates between 80 to 100 feet, formed when strong water currents from hurricanes and storms washed sand from offshore shoals onto the beach. Over many years the wind picked up the sand and blew it inland. Those tiny grains of sand formed the dunes that now stretch for many miles along the coastline.

Much of the Outer Banks has been developed, so this massive sand mountain is both rare and memorable. When bulldozers appeared on the sound side of the dunes in the 1970s, local residents organized a "People to Preserve Jockey's Ridge" campaign that eventually led to the creation of the state park in 1975.

Although the dunes' unstable ridges are barren of plant life, maritime thickets grow at the base of the dunes and between the dune field and Roanoke Sound. These thickets contain wax myrtle, red cedar, live oak, and bayberry and offer a rest stop for migrating warblers during the fall. Most park visitors like to

CONTACT INFO

West Carolista Drive
Nags Head, NC 27959
Phone: (252) 441-7132
Fax: (252) 441-8416
E-mail:
jockeys.ridge@ncmail.net

LOCATION Jockey's Ridge State Park is located in Dare County on the Outer Banks. The entrance to the park, Carolista Drive, is on the left after the town of Nags Head on the US 158 Bypass (South Croatan Highway).

SIZE 426 acres

GPS 35.9600, -75.6326

scramble up the dunes to get the expansive perspective of the coastline, but two trails at the dunes' base offer a different view of life in a dune field. The one-mile Soundside Trail passes through maritime thicket and wetland areas, while the 1.5-mile Tracks in the Sand trail focuses on the imprints left by creatures that are often unseen by park visitors: fox, insects, and snakes.

Jockey's Ridge offers a good vantage point to view migrating raptors like sharp-shinned hawks and kestrels in the fall. If you're more into people-powered aviation, you probably know that Jockey's Ridge is a popular hang-gliding spot for people with a USHGA Hang I or equivalent card. You must register with the park office.

Stop by the visitor center to learn more about the dunes and check out a display of fulgurites – glass tubes formed when lightning strikes sand and "freezes." Friends of Jockey's Ridge supports the park. Visit www.jockeysridgestatepark.com.

Staying Alive
Wear shoes to protect your feet from hot sand, and stay out of hang-gliding areas.

Nearby
- The Nature Conservancy's Nags Head Woods Preserve is adjacent to Jockey's Ridge. A barrier of ancient dunes that includes Jockey's Ridge and Run Hill, a 123-acre State Natural Area, protect this rare maritime forest from salt spray. Visit www.nature.org/northcarolina.
- Alligator River National Wildlife Refuge: www.fws.gov/alligatorriver
- Cape Hatteras National Seashore: www.nps.gov/caha
- Pea Island National Wildlife Refuge: www.fws.gov/peaisland

JONES LAKE STATE PARK/
SINGLETARY LAKE STATE PARK

Jones Lake State Park is probably best known as a great spot for swimming and fishing, yet Jones Lake and Salters Lake, both contained in this park, are also significant because they are among the few protected Carolina bays remaining in the Southeast. Carolina bays are oval, shallow lakes that were once common fixtures in the region, but today most of them have been drained or filled for agricultural use. Other bays in the state parks system are Bay Tree, Bushy Lake, Singletary, and Lake Waccamaw, and each of them offers visitors an opportunity to explore the geology of Carolina bays and enjoy their unique flora.

CONTACT INFO

4117 NC 242 Highway North
Elizabethtown, NC 28337
Phone: (910) 588-4550
Fax: (910) 588-4322
E-mail: jones.lake@ncmail.net

Carolina bays are named for the loblolly, red, and Virginia bay trees that grow around them. At Jones Lake, insect-eating pitcher plants and sundews thrive in the wet pocosin areas and sunny fringes. Turkey oaks and remnant longleaf pines, an archetypal symbol of the southern landscape, grow on upland sandy ridges. To explore the bay flora and fauna, take the Bay Trail, a three-mile trail that loops around the lake and passes by pond cypress festooned with Spanish moss. Follow some of the side trails to get a closer look at the lake and with patience, you may spot some of

LOCATION	These two parks are in different sections of the 36,000-acre Bladen Lakes State Forest, in Bladen County. Jones Lake lies four miles north of Elizabethtown on NC 242, and Singletary Lake is about six miles east of Elizabethtown on NC 53.
SIZE	Jones Lake State Park (includes Salters Lake State Natural Area): 1,984 acres; Singletary Lake State Park: 649 acres
GPS	Jones Lake: 34.6810, -78.5959; Singletary Lake: 34.5831, -78.4496

the tiny amphibians that dwell here, like spring peeper and southern leopard frog. Early morning and late afternoon are good times to look for some of the park's resident birds, such as pileated woodpecker, and in the breeding season, migratory birds like wood thrush.

You can rent a canoe or paddleboat at Jones Lake, or launch your own small boat. In warm weather, you might enjoy a dip in the cool tea-colored water. A bathhouse offers showers and restrooms. The park's visitor center features interpretive exhibits about Carolina bays.

Nearby Salters Lake is managed by the park as a natural area, and you need a permit from park staff to visit it. Because there is only one access road to Salters Lake and no trails, the best way to explore the bay is in a canoe or kayak. Look for the endangered red cockaded woodpecker, which nests in colonies in old-growth pines around the lake. The park is in the process of expanding the trail system at Jones Lake to connect to Salters.

continued next page

Singletary Lake

Singletary Lake is reserved for group camping and offers two camps for nonprofit youth and adult organizations. Camp Ipecac houses 88 campers and is named for a medicinal herb that grows nearby and is possibly used as an antidote for dining hall cuisine. Camp Loblolly Bay houses 48 campers. Each camp includes dining halls, cabins, restrooms, and almost everything else, except food, cleaning supplies, and bed linens.

Campers enjoy the serenity of a protected natural area, as well as boating, hiking, fishing, swimming, and an education center. Only Camp Loblolly Bay is open year round. Contact the main park office to make reservations.

Staying Alive

Like all Carolina bays, these lakes are shallow: do not dive into them from piers or boats.

Nearby

- Lake Waccamaw State Park: See page 96.
- Lumber River State Park: See page 98.

The Carolina Bay Mystery

The North Carolina state map shows dozens of small lakes scattered throughout the southeastern section of the state, all oriented northwest to southeast. These are the Carolina bays, and Bladen County features many of them: Bakers, Carver's, Horseshoe, Jones, Little Singletary, Moores, Salters, Singletary, and White Lakes. There are many theories about how the bays were formed; among the proposed causes are whale wallows, extraterrestrials, meteor showers, or (more mundane, but perhaps more plausible), wind and water currents.

Carolina bays became more widely known when the first aerial photos of the region taken in the 1930s revealed strange pockmarks on the landscape. Geologists estimate that there were once more than a half-million Carolina bays scattered along the east coast. They are all encircled by a sand ridge that is most pronounced on the southeast side. Bays are often lined with a clay layer that retains moisture, while sand and dense vegetation extend around their perimeters. They are shallow, ranging from 8 to 12 feet in depth, and typically rain-fed. They range in size from less than an acre to several thousand acres. As sediments and organic material slowly penetrate the lake, if they are left undisturbed, they can eventually develop into moist bogs. Most Carolina bays have been drained for farming and development, although public and private conservation groups have been working to protect the most ecologically significant examples.

So what's your theory of their formation?

LAKE WACCAMAW STATE PARK

Lake Waccamaw lures visitors with the serenity of its clear water and surrounding forestland. Thousands of Carolina bays like Waccamaw dot the coastal plain, but this quirk of nature is the largest water-filled bay lake in North Carolina. (See Jones Lake State Park, page 92.)

Like most Carolina bays, Lake Waccamaw is a shallow, oval depression (averaging seven feet in depth), oriented northwest to southeast. While most bays are rain-fed, Waccamaw is fed by Big Creek, which empties into the bay from the north. On the southern side of the lake, the lake drains into the Waccamaw River, which is flanked by extensive swamp forests.

One of the most biologically important bodies of water in the eastern United States, Lake Waccamaw supports a remarkable diversity of plants and animals, particularly mollusk and fish species that are found nowhere else in the world. Many bay lakes are acidic, but limestone outcrops on the northeast shore of this lake neutralize the water, making it a hospitable environment for aquatic life. Mussels, snails, and fish thrive here because of the

CONTACT INFO

1866 State Park Drive
Lake Waccamaw, NC 28450
Phone: (910) 646-4748
Fax: (910) 646-4915
E-mail:
lake.waccamaw@ncmail.net

LOCATION	The park is in Columbus County, 38 miles west of Wilmington and 12 miles east of Whiteville, off NC 214.
SIZE	1,756 acres, including the 8,938-acre lake
GPS	34.2555, -78.5001

excellent quality of the water and its neutral pH. You can see the fish and mussels "in action" in a video in the visitor's center.

Lake Waccamaw is part of a large wildlife corridor that includes the Green Swamp. Although you would be lucky to see them, wary bobcats and black bears inhabit the area. American alligators occasionally surface in the lake and in roadside canals near the park. The rare Brimley's chorus frog is a park resident, and spring evenings are full of the sounds of spring peepers and cricket frogs.

Visitors can explore the park on several hiking trails, including the five-mile Lake Trail, which wanders through pine forest and cypress trees. Stop for a picnic at sandy beaches along the way, or camp in one of the park's four primitive group camping sites. A 700-foot boardwalk penetrates the Bay Forest, a good place for birdlife, while a 375-foot pier offers a relaxing place to do some fishing. Although the park does not have a boat launch, the N.C. Wildlife Resources Commission and Columbus County manage public boat ramps on the east and west sides of the lake.

Staying Alive
Wear a life jacket while boating, and watch out for strong winds that can whip up big waves on the lake.

Nearby
- Jones Lake State Park: See 92.
- Green Swamp Preserve: nature.org/northcarolina

LUMBER RIVER STATE PARK

A canoeing and kayaking paradise, the Lumber is the only blackwater river in North Carolina to be designated a Wild and Scenic River. Nowadays, it may be hard to believe that the Lumber once supported a busy logging community, the industry that probably gave the river its name. The river was a busy highway for commerce in the 18th century, but today few roads access the upper and lower reaches, giving that stretch a real wilderness feel. The middle section of the river around Lumberton is more heavily used.

CONTACT INFO

2819 Princess Ann Road
Orrum, NC 28369
Phone: (910) 628-9844
Fax: (910) 628-1185
E-mail:
lumber.river@ncmail.net

Consult the Lumber River home page on the state parks Web site for paddling routes and a map. The park offers boat access along the upper stretches of the river and canoe camping at Chalk Banks and Jasper Landing. Paddling from SR 2121, you can camp at Buck Landing, Piney Island, and Pea Ridge, and take out at the park office at Princess Ann Landing. Princess Ann was the second town chartered in Robeson County because it offered the safety of a high bluff and a good landing spot.

LOCATION The Lumber River State Park is in Columbus and Robeson Counties; the park headquarters is in Robeson County, south of Lumberton, in the Princess Ann Access Area. The other main access areas are upriver, at Buck Landing, Piney Island, and Pea Ridge.

SIZE 8,274 acres, and 15 miles along the Lumber River

GPS 34.3887, -79.0028

Take your time paddling the clear, tea-colored river. You may see hummingbirds feeding on wild azaleas or hear barred owls calling from the bald cypress and tulip poplars at night. In springtime the banks of the river come alive with blooming mountain laurel and spider lilies. Birders have reported seeing anhingas and Mississippi kites flying over the river. The park's bird list stands at 160 species and growing. If you are without a boat, check out the nature trail at Princess Ann landing.

Staying Alive
Contact the park office to check on river conditions before paddling and wear a life jacket while on the water.

Nearby
· Lake Waccamaw State Park: See page 96.

"I've been lost and I've been found"

A trip along the Lumber teaches patience. It's different from a white-water experience, where a glance away from the water while you're lurching through rapids can spell disaster. Here, you dawdle. You can pull onto a sandbar for a break, and look overhead to see barred owls looking back at you. Sometimes you may have to stop altogether to drag your canoe over a log draped in poison ivy.

Around Boardman, just when you believe the river corridor can't get any narrower, it fans out into pools and rivulets, and you only know that you are heading downstream by carefully inspecting the water flow. As you paddle around the old trestles from the logging operations of yesteryear, you might imagine yourself in a lost wilderness. Until you hear the trucks whining over the Highway 64 bridge ahead. – Bill Pendergraft

MASONBORO ISLAND STATE NATURAL AREA

f you have access to a boat and want to spend some time wandering around an undeveloped barrier island, Masonboro Island near Wrightsville Beach is worth a visit. This eight-mile-long narrow spit offers classic coastal habitats: open beach, dunes, maritime grassland, and marsh. Located between Wrightsville Beach and Carolina Beach, the island is a great destination for fishing, beach-combing, birding, and swimming. The low-lying island is frequently overwashed during storms and most of the island is comprised of tidal flats and extensive marsh.

Anglers report that this is a good spot at the appropriate time of year for mullet, bluefish, and spot. Although there are more accessible places along the southeastern coast for birding, such as Carolina Beach State Park and Fort Fisher State Recreation Area, if you have a boat and extra time, a trip here can turn up some enjoyable finds. Wilson's plover, least tern, and black skimmer nest here. The mud flats are good places to scan for shorebirds. In the late fall and winter, check the ocean for gannets and loons.

Nearby
- Carolina Beach State Park: See page 68.
- Fort Fisher State Recreation Area: See page 80.

LOCATION	New Hanover County
SIZE	106 acres
GPS	34.1342, -77.8466

MERCHANTS MILLPOND STATE PARK

R ural North Carolina is dotted with remnant mills that seeded local communities. Early settlers built water-powered mills for sawing lumber and grinding corn and wheat. Entrepreneurs often capitalized on the mill's traffic by building their own businesses nearby. These business complexes served as social centers for growing communities; people gathered in these places to trade, gossip, and fish, or take a dip in the cool millpond. So it was in Gates County as Norfleets Millpond, built in 1811, grew into an early retail center, and the millpond came to be known as Merchants Millpond. Millponds became important wildlife sanctuaries as well; when beavers were nearly trapped to extinction in North Carolina, these ponds offered wetland habitats for plants and animals that had previously relied on beaver ponds.

As you paddle across the pond you weave through cypress and tupelo gum trees draped in Spanish moss. Cow lilies and floating mats of duckweed cover the black water. Paddlers can drift into Lassiter Swamp at the head of the pond, where they will find a grove of virgin cypress trees thought to be 1,000 years old.

CONTACT INFO
71 US Highway 158 East
Gatesville, NC 27938
Phone: (252) 357-1191
Fax: (252) 357-0149
E-mail: merchants.millpond@ncmail.net

LOCATION   Merchants Millpond State Park is near the town of Gatesville, in Gates County, approximately 30 miles from Ahoskie, Elizabeth City, and Edenton, and 30 miles from Suffolk, Virginia.

SIZE   3,296 acres

GPS   36.4399, -76.6724

The park's animal life is legion. You will hear the noisy calls of leopard, cricket, and chorus frogs in the springtime and see turtles like yellow-bellied sliders basking on logs. The park boasts an impressive bird list: 210 species to date. Keep an eye out for pileated woodpeckers throughout the year and waterfowl in the fall and winter. Paddlers can follow a marked canoe trail to two canoe campsites, for camping overnight or just picnicking and resting. You can bring your own boat or rent canoes at the park. More than nine miles of hiking trails wander around the edge of the millpond and Lassiter Swamp. Lassiter Trail leads to five backpack camping sites and the park also offers a drive-in family campground. A new visitor center was being developed for the park when this guide went to press.

Staying Alive

Ticks are abundant in warmer months, so avoid them by dressing accordingly and using insect repellent. Beware too, of venomous snakes and poison ivy.

Nearby

- Dismal Swamp State Park: See page 76.
- Great Dismal Swamp National Wildlife Refuge: www.fws.gov/northeast/greatdismalswamp/

Diving Merchants Millpond

When Environmental Media was filming the North Carolina Public Television series *Wild, NC,* the superintendent at Merchants Millpond gave our film crew permission to take underwater video footage of the pond. Although the tannic water of the millpond seems quite opaque from above, the visibility under the surface is in fact excellent.

We landed our canoes on the north bank and swam out, underwater video cameras in hand, heading for a big cypress tree. Overhead, we could see the noon sun flashing through the water, the floating lilies and duckweed, and the moss-draped green canopy. We circled the cypress trunk underwater to explore the tree's protruding knees, and small fish came over to have a look. As the bottom is thick with decayed vegetation, we were careful not to kick, as it would have filled the water with debris and visibility would have dropped to zero.

If there were any water snakes in the area, they had skedaddled. We swam into deeper open water. Here it felt like swimming in a gigantic pitcher of tea, as the bottom dropped away, and looking down, we stared into the darker brown shadows below. – Bill Pendergraft

Pettigrew State Park is defined by water, both black and clear. The park's centerpiece is rain-fed clearwater Lake Phelps, at five miles wide the second largest lake in North Carolina. This shallow lake averages only 4.5 feet in depth, and 9 feet at its deepest. A new section of the park protects a stretch of swamp forest along the blackwater Scuppernong River, which flows out of the lake.

Most park visitors are drawn to water-related activities. Motorboats, canoes, kayaks, and sailboats all share the water. The lake is renowned for its largemouth bass, yellow perch, and sunfish. Walking or biking the park's nine miles of trails is a perfect way to experience the old-growth forests surrounding the lake. The 2.8-mile Moccasin Trail starts at the park office and leads you through a cypress and hardwood forest where you can look for woodpeckers and raptors. The trail ends at a 350-foot boardwalk that offers a stunning view of the lake.

Pettigrew is a great place for migratory birds during the spring and summer, among them warblers, tanagers, yellow-billed cuckoo, and wood thrush. Tundra swans and snow geese migrate here in

CONTACT INFO

2252 Lake Shore Road
Creswell, NC 27928
Phone: (252) 797-4475
Fax: (252) 797-7405
E-mail: pettigrew@ncmail.net

LOCATION The park is seven miles south of Creswell off US 64, in Washington and Tyrrell Counties.

SIZE 3,182 acres of land, 16,600 acres of lake

GPS 35.8312, -76.3834

the fall, and their calls from the interior of the lake can be otherworldly on a gray winter day. Campers at the park sleep beneath giant bald cypress, and on clear nights, they enjoy a sky free of light pollution.

Pettigrew is famous for its virgin forest – some of the cypress trees here have been dated at 800 years old. The park is home to record-setting sweetbay and loblolly bay trees. Many of the park's huge trees were toppled during Hurricane Isabel in 2003, including the state's two national champion trees. However, the park is still home to at least four species of trees that measure over 4.5 feet in diameter. The park holds a Big Tree Walk every November to take visitors to some of the behemoths.

The Scuppernong section of the park is a tranquil destination for paddlers and anglers. The river and surrounding swamp forests are home to at least 60 species of breeding birds, including 13 species of warblers, as well as black bear and red wolf. A paddling map is available on the park Web site.

Staying Alive
While boating, be aware of natural hazards such as snags, wind, and waves.

Nearby
- Palmetto-Peartree Preserve: www.palmettopeartree.org
- Pocosin Lakes National Wildlife Refuge: www.fws.gov/pocosinlakes/

Stories from the Past

Before the development of rail and highway networks, rivers like the Scuppernong connected landlocked farmers and plantation owners to outside markets. Just after the American Revolution, Edenton merchant Josiah Collins and two companions formed the Lake Company and acquired approximately 100,000 acres between Lake Phelps and the Scuppernong, with the intention of draining the lake and converting the swamp land to agricultural uses. The company squeezed agricultural riches out of swampland, but only at the expense of enslaved Africans and the health of the natural landscape.

Slaves dug several canals that connected lakes to the Scuppernong River and drained the swampland around the lake, making virgin forest accessible for lumbering. The canals enabled landowners and farmers to deliver wheat, corn, rice, lumber and other products to sailing vessels anchored in the Scuppernong. The river commerce supported three antebellum plantations in the area, including Somerset Place on the shores of Lake Phelps. You can visit Somerset Place State Historic Site, adjacent to Pettigrew State Park. Visit www.ah.dcr.state.nc.us/sections/hs/somerset/somerset.htm.

WEYMOUTH WOODS SANDHILLS NATURE PRESERVE

North Carolina's Sandhills region has long been famous as a golfing mecca. However, when you see the longleaf pines and white sandy soils in places like Weymouth Woods, you know that there is something here for the naturalist as well. The Sandhills are thought to be an ancient delta that was formed by streams flowing eastward toward the ocean. The landscape is rolling, with gentle sandy ridges and broad valleys. Years of fire suppression and harvesting have greatly diminished the longleaf pine forests that once dominated the region. These forests once extended over 90 million acres from Virginia to Texas, but today they cover only about 4 percent of their original range.

CONTACT INFO

1024 Fort Bragg Road
Southern Pines, NC 28387
Phone: (910) 692-2167
Fax: (910) 692-8042
E-mail: weymouth.woods@
ncmail.net

The preserve's 4.5 miles of trails take you through various habitats. On the uplands you walk through open longleaf forest with some scrub oaks and an understory of wiregrass, the plant that helps fire circulate through the forest. Look for V-shaped incisions on the pine trunks: these are scars from historical sap-tapping to produce turpentine and other naval stores. Seeps carpeted in sphagnum moss and streamhead pocosins occur on the slopes, and a mixed hardwood/pine forest grows along streams.

LOCATION	The preserve is located off US 1, two miles east of Southern Pines, in Moore County.
SIZE	900 acres
GPS	35.1530, -79.3671

The Bower's Bog Trail takes you from the visitor center to an upland bog with pitcher plants; the 1-mile Pine Barrens Trail goes through an open longleaf forest; while the 0.5-mile Gum Swamp Trail loops off this trail and travels through a swampy area around James Creek. The Pine Island Trail crosses over several creeks on boardwalks and passes through a hardwood forest where pileated woodpeckers are often heard drumming.

Watch for the distinctively marked pine barrens treefrog, and the fox squirrel, a larger relative of the gray squirrel, with a black head, feet, and tail. A colony of red-cockaded woodpeckers nests near the visitor's center from about mid-April through May. This federally endangered species depends on old longleaf pines for foraging and nesting. All told, 167 bird species have been seen at the preserve.

From about February through November you can enjoy a variety of flowering plants, including pitcher plants, orchids, and asters. Park staff conducts prescribed burns throughout the year to mimic the natural lightning-ignited fires that knock back understory plants.

Staying Alive
Be wary of the usual summertime hazards of ticks and chiggers.

Nearby
· Sandhills Game Lands: The game lands are an exceptional place for observing the plants, birds, and butterflies of the Sandhills. They are open for hunting at certain times of year, and year-round for hiking, mountain biking (you need fat tires), and horseback riding. Visit www.ncwildlife.org.

Insect Eaters

Who could not be intrigued by a plant that "eats" insects? Charles Darwin proclaimed the Venus flytrap "one of the most wonderful [plants] in the world," and the many other species of carnivorous plants, including pitcher plants and sundews, are just as fascinating. Insect-eating plants grow in acidic, nutrient-poor soil and developed the ability to capture and digest insects to supplement their diet. Insects that fall prey to pitcher plants slide down into a water-filled pool called a pitfall trap where the plant slowly digests them with enzymes. Carnivorous plants face many challenges: they typically grow in dwindling wetland habitats and are often targeted by plant poachers.

niche publishing llc

Niche produces media that explores the relationships between people and place. Niche illuminates the world's undiscovered places and conservation issues. We help people find their place in natural and cultural communities.

Niche Guides are written for thoughtful travelers who are eager to explore unique, uncrowded destinations. The guides appeal to all types of outdoor adventurers, from Sunday drivers prowling dusty backroads in the family sedan, to wilderness fanatics who thrive on people-free haunts. Niche Guides are written for people who want to immerse themselves in the nooks and crannies of the world – those niches that make our planet so diverse.

Niche Publishing LLC is a partnership between Ida Phillips Lynch and Bill Pendergraft.

Ida Phillips Lynch is an environmental writer and the author of *The Duke Forest at 75: A Resource for All Seasons* and *North Carolina Afield*. She is a frequent contributor to *Wildlife in North Carolina*. The communications coordinator for Triangle Land Conservancy in Raleigh, NC, Ida was formerly the director of communications for The Nature Conservancy, NC Chapter.

Contact: idalynch@envmedia.com, (919) 618-0631

Writer/producer **Bill Pendergraft** is the founder of Environmental Media, an 18-year-old company that designs and produces media to support environmental education. The company has written and produced more than 500 award-winning guides, programs, and series including *Wild, NC*, a 20-program series on North Carolina State Parks for UNC-TV. See www.envmedia.com.

Contact: bpendergraft@envmedia.com

Visit www.nichepress.com for the latest news and titles from Niche Publishing.

friends of state parks

Friends of State Parks (FSP) is a non-profit citizen's group formed in 1973 that is dedicated to the understanding, enjoyment, and protection of North Carolina's State Parks. Its mission is to support the N.C. Division of Parks and Recreation in its work to protect and manage the unique biological, geological, archaeological, recreational, and scenic resources of the state. FSP promotes public awareness of the immense contributions of these natural areas to the quality of life for North Carolinians.

For more information and to join FSP visit http://ncfsp.org.

North Carolina State Parks Map Guide

In 2007, FSP published the *North Carolina State Parks Map Guide.* This 121-page comprehensive guide has park maps and information for all active parks and natural areas as well as information on parks under development.

The 8.5" x 11" coil bound book works as a coffee table book for trip planning and as a backpack reference guide. To view sample contents and order the book visit the FSP Web site: http://ncfsp.org.

Some individual state parks also have a Friends Group that operates as a support arm for the park.

Eno River Association
4419 Guess Road
Durham, NC 27712
Phone: (919) 620-9099
www.enoriver.org

Falls Lake – B.W. Wells Association
PO Box 1901
Wake Forest, NC 27588
www.bwwells.org

Friends of Crowders Mountain State Park
PO Box 1881
Gastonia, NC 28053
www.friendsofcrowdersmountain.org

Friends of Fort Macon
PO Box 651
Beaufort, NC 28516
www.clis.com/friends

Friends of Goose Creek State Park
2190 Camp Leach Road
Washington, NC 27889

Friends of Hammocks and Bear Island
PO Box 1861
Swansboro, NC 28584

Friends of Jockey's Ridge
PO Box 358
Nags Head, NC 27959
www.jockeysridgestatepark.com

Friends of Lake Waccamaw State Park
809 Pecan Lane
Lake Waccamaw, NC 28450

National Audubon Society, Elisha Mitchell Chapter (Mount Mitchell)
PO Box 18711
Asheville, NC 28814
www.main.nc.us/emas/

The Umstead Coalition
PO Box 10654
Raleigh, NC 27605
Phone: (919) 852-2268
http://umsteadcoalition.org

conservation community in north carolina

Public Agencies

N.C. Division of Parks and Recreation
1615 MSC
Raleigh, NC 27699
Phone: (919) 733-4181
www.ncparks.gov

For general information about state parks or to request a state park brochure, call (919) 733-PARK or e-mail parkinfo@ncmail.net.

N.C. Department of Environment and Natural Resources
DENR Customer Service Center
1640 MSC
Raleigh, NC 27699-1640
Phone: (877) 623-6748
www.enr.state.nc.us

The N.C. Department of Environment and Natural Resources (DENR) is the lead stewardship agency for the protection of North Carolina's outstanding natural resources.

N.C. Division of Coastal Management
400 Commerce Avenue
Morehead City, NC 28557
Phone: 1-888-4RCOAST
http://dcm2.enr.state.nc.us

The N.C. Division of Coastal Management oversees the Coastal Reserve system to ensure the preservation of natural resources and threatened habitat in North Carolina's twenty coastal counties. These public natural areas provide wildlife viewing and coastal kayaking opportunities.

N.C. Natural Heritage Program
1601 MSC
Raleigh, NC 27699
Phone: (919) 715-4195
www.ncnhp.org

The N.C. Natural Heritage Program inventories, catalogues, and supports conservation of the rarest and the most outstanding elements of North Carolina's natural diversity. The program works with a variety of private organizations, individuals, corporations, and public agencies.

N.C. Wildlife Resources Commission (North Carolina Game Lands)

1751 Varsity Drive
NCSU Centennial Campus
Raleigh, NC 27606
Phone: (919) 707-0010
www.ncwildlife.org

The North Carolina Wildlife Resources Commission (WRC) is dedicated to the conservation and management of the state's fish and wildlife resources. Wildlife Commission game lands are open for a variety of recreational activities, including hiking, hunting, and fishing. Game land maps are accessible on the WRC Web site. Trails in game lands are often not well-marked.

U.S. Fish and Wildlife Service (National Wildlife Refuges)

www.fws.gov

The mission of USFWS is to work with others to conserve, protect and enhance fish, wildlife and plants and their habitats. The service manages the 93 million-acre National Wildlife Refuge System. Visit the USFWS Web site for a list of refuges and contact information for North Carolina.

U.S. Forest Service (National Forests)

160A Zillicoa Street, Asheville
NC 28801
Phone: (828) 257-4200
www.cs.unca.edu/nfsnc

National Forest property in North Carolina includes Nantahala, Pisgah, Croatan, and Uwharrie National Forests. Most of this land is open for hiking, hunting, fishing, and camping.

N.C. Division of Forest Resources

DENR
1616 MSC
Raleigh, NC 27699-1616
Phone: (919) 733-2162
www.dfr.state.nc.us

The Division of Forest Resources protects, manages, and conserves the forest resources of the state. The Division of Forest Resources is directly involved with forest management assistance to private landowners, reforestation services, forest fire prevention and suppression, and insect and disease control programs.

Nonprofit Organizations

This is not a comprehensive listing, but a listing of many groups that partner with the N.C. Division of Parks and Recreation.

Audubon North Carolina

123 Kingston Drive, Suite 206A
Chapel Hill, NC 27514-1651
Phone: (919) 929-3899
www.ncaudubon.org

Audubon North Carolina's mission is to conserve and restore North Carolina's ecosystems, focusing on the needs of birds. Audubon North Carolina has 10,500 members and 7 chapters across the state.

Carolina Bird Club

6325 Falls of the Neuse Road
STE 9 PMB 150
Raleigh, NC 27615
www.carolinabirdclub.org

The Carolina Bird Club is a nonprofit educational and scientific association that was founded in 1937. The best way to keep up with interesting bird sightings in North Carolina is to join a listserv such the one sponsored by CBC, called Carolinabirds. Visit the Web site for more information.

Conservation Trust for North Carolina

1028 Washington Street
Raleigh, NC 27605
Phone: (919) 828-4199
www.ctnc.org

The mission of CTNC is to protect North Carolina's land and water through statewide conservation and cooperative work with land trusts. CTNC is an umbrella group for the state's land trusts, many of which collaborate with the N.C. Division of Parks and Recreation on conservation projects. Visit the Web site to obtain contact information for all of North Carolina's land trusts.

Mountains to Sea Trail

3585 US 401-South
Louisburg, NC 27549
www.ncmst.org

North Carolina's Mountains to Sea Trail (MST) is a 900+ mile trail consisting of footpaths, roads, and state bike routes. When completed, the MST will extend from Clingman's Dome in the Great Smoky Mountains National Park to Jockey's Ridge State Park on the Outer Banks. Currently the trail passes through the following state parks and state recreation areas: Eno River, Falls Lake, Hanging Rock, Jockey's Ridge, Mount Mitchell, Pilot Mountain, and Stone Mountain. Plans call for the trail to eventually pass through Cliffs of the Neuse and Haw River State Parks.

N.C. Paddle Trails Association

600 Lancaster Road
Pikeville, NC 27863
www.ncpaddletrails.org

The mission of the N.C. Paddle Trails Association is to empower communities in the local development, maintenance, and restoration of paddle trails in North Carolina.

North Carolina Birding Trail

NC Wildlife Resources Commission
1722 Mail Service Center
Raleigh, NC 27699-1722
Phone: (919) 604-5183
www.ncbirdingtrail.org

The North Carolina Birding Trail is a cooperative effort to link bird watching sites and birders with communities, businesses, and other local historical and educational attractions in North Carolina. The trail is complete in the coastal plain and the piedmont and mountain sections will be completed in the future. Many N.C. State Parks are included on the trail.

The Nature Conservancy

N.C. Chapter
4705 University Drive, Suite 290
Durham, NC 27707
Phone: (919) 403-8558
nature.org/northcarolina

The mission of The Nature Conservancy is to preserve the plants, animals and natural communities that represent the diversity of life on Earth by protecting the lands and waters they need to survive. This global organization works in all 50 states and in 27 countries. The Nature Conservancy, North Carolina Chapter partners with the N.C. Division of Parks and Recreation on many conservation projects.

Funding Sources

N.C. Clean Water Management Trust Fund

651 Mail Service Center
Raleigh, NC 27699-1651
Phone: (919) 733-6375
www.cwmtf.net

The 1996 General Assembly of North Carolina established the Clean Water Management Trust Fund (CWMTF) to help local governments, state agencies, and conservation nonprofit groups finance projects to protect and restore surface water quality. Thanks to appropriations from the General Assembly, the CWMTF has awarded 943 grants for a total of $711.5 million to date.

N.C. Parks and Recreation Trust Fund

1615 MSC
Raleigh, NC 27699-1615
Phone: (919) 715-2662
www.partf.net

The North Carolina General Assembly established the Parks and Recreation Trust Fund (PARTF) in 1994 to fund improvements in the state's park system, to fund grants for local government, and to increase the public's access to beaches. PARTF is the primary source of funding to build and renovate facilities in state parks and to buy land for new and existing parks.

N.C. Natural Heritage Trust Fund

1601 MSC
Raleigh, NC 27699
Phone: (919) 715-8014
www.nchntf.org

The North Carolina Natural Heritage Trust fund provides supplemental funding to select state agencies to acquire and protect important natural areas, preserve the state's ecological diversity and cultural heritage, and inventory the state's natural heritage resources. The trust fund is supported by 25% of the state's portion of the tax on real estate deed transfers and by a portion of the fees for personalized license plates. These sources now generate about $19 million each year. Since its creation in 1987, the trust fund has contributed more than $194 million to support the conservation of more than 251,000 acres.

the best of....
in north carolina state parks

A completely biased guide

Mountains
- Elk Knob: Best mountaintop for contemplating the journey of life and feeling good about making it to the top.
- Gorges: Best great big place to lose yourself. You can hike here until your boots fall off.
- Mount Mitchell: Best natural high. Can you see the Black Hills of South Dakota yet?
- New River: Best paddle/kayak for a beginner, although we turned over there.
- Stone Mountain: Best trout fishing, I hear.

Piedmont
- Eno River: Best urban park. Our Girl Scout troop stopped talking for a few minutes there.
- Hanging Rock: Most beautiful lake. Forget the rock and check out the lake.
- Morrow Mountain: Best swimming pool, and only swimming pool, and don't forget to check out Dr. Kron's house.
- Raven Rock: Best place to sit on a big rock, and watch a big river flow by.
- South Mountains: Best wilderness area in the Piedmont.

Coastal Plain
- Goose Creek: Bill's favorite park in North Carolina.
- Hammocks Beach: Best place to see a loggerhead sea turtle and the fewest people.
- Lake Waccamaw: Best dock on a Carolina Bay. Bring your Sunfish.
- Lumber River: Best paddle/kayak trip in North Carolina hands down.
- Merchants Millpond: Best park for a relaxing paddle in an old millpond.
- Pettigrew State Park: Best place to camp under gigantic cypress trees.
- Weymouth Woods: Best place to imagine what the Southeast used to look like and see North Carolina's state tree.

Ida Phillips Lynch and Bill Pendergraft

naturally wonderful state parks license plate

The N.C. Division of Parks and Recreation is now accepting applications and checks for the first 300 North Carolina State Parks license plates. In addition to supporting the state parks system by displaying this license plate, a portion of the sale will benefit the Parks and Recreation and Natural Heritage Trust Funds. The Parks Division must receive a minimum of 300 applications with payment in advance prior to submitting to DMV. Once DMV receives the initial order, processing and delivery of the new plates should occur within 90 days. After receiving the minimum 300 applications, plates will be produced and mailed directly from DMV. Plates can be purchased for "weighted" vehicles (including buses and camping trailers) from 7,000 pounds up to 26,000 pounds. The plate will not be marked weighted, but the registration will indicate its status. For more information and to order a plate, visit the N.C. State Parks Web site: www.ncparks.gov.

further reading

Bearden, Karen, Ed. *Birding in North Carolina State Parks.* Chapel Hill: Audubon North Carolina, 2002.

Biggs, Walter C., Jr. and James F. Parnell. *State Parks of North Carolina.* Winston-Salem: John F. Blair, 1995.

Brooks, Marshall and Mark Johns, Eds. *Birding North Carolina.* Guilford: The Globe Pequot Press, 2005.

Delorme. *North Carolina Atlas & Gazetteer.* Yarmouth: Delorme Mapping Company, 2006.

Frankenberg, Dirk, Ed. *Exploring North Carolina's Natural Areas.* Chapel Hill: The University of North Carolina Press, 2000.

—. *The Nature of North Carolina's Southern Coast: Barrier Islands, Coastal Waters, and Wetlands.* Chapel Hill: The University of North Carolina Press, 1997.

Fussell, John O. III. *A Birder's Guide to Coastal North Carolina.* Chapel Hill: The University of North Carolina Press, 1994.

Johnson, Randy. *Hiking North Carolina.* Guilford: The Globe Pequot Press, 2007.

Lynch, Ida Phillips. *North Carolina Afield: A Guide to Nature Conservancy Projects in North Carolina.* Durham: The Nature Conservancy, N.C. Chapter, 2002.

Manuel, John. *The Natural Traveler Along North Carolina's Coast.* Winston-Salem: John F. Blair, Publisher, 2003.

N.C. Center for Geographic Information & Analysis. *North Carolina Coastal Plain Paddle Trails Guide.* NCCPPTI, 2001. www.ncsu.edu/paddletrails.

N.C. Wildlife Resources Commission. *Wildlife in North Carolina.* www.ncwildlife.org.

notes

notes

Photo Credits

All the photos in this book were taken by Ida Phillips Lynch and Bill Pendergraft of Niche Publishing LLC, except for the following. Many of the Niche photos are for sale at www.nichepress.com.

Many thanks to these photographers for their wonderful work.

Hammocks Beach State Park (Front cover and p. 89): Ken Taylor
Chimney Rock State Park (pp. 12-13): N.C. Division of Parks and Recreation (NCDPR)
Gorges State Park (pp. 16-17): Jere Snyder
Lake James State Park (pp. 18-19): NCDPR
Mt. Mitchell State Park (pp. 22-23): NCDPR
Stone Mountain State Park (pp. 26-27): Jere Snyder
Deep River State Trail (p. 33): NCDPR
Eno River State Park (p. 34, far right): Eno River Association
Jordan Lake State Recreation Area (p. 45): NCDPR
Kerr Lake State Recreation Area (p. 46-47): NCDPR
Lower Haw River State Natural Area (pp. 50-51): NCDPR
South Mountains State Park (p. 62, middle): NCDPR
South Mountains State Park (pp. 62-63): Jere Snyder
Hammocks Beach State Park (p. 88): NCDPR
Jockey's Ridge State Park (pp. 90-91): NCDPR
Singletary Lake State Park (p. 92, far right): NCDPR
Lumber River State Park (p. 98, far right, and p. 99): NCDPR